BLOOMFIELD TOWNSHIP PUBLIC LIBRARY

3 1160 00505 6226

W9-BXE-220

BLOOMFIELD TOWNSHIP PUBLIC LIBRARY
1099 Lone Pine Road
Bloomfield Hills, Michigan 48302-2410

SOUL

OF

NOWHERE

SOUL

OF

NOWHERE

TRAVERSING GRACE IN A RUGGED LAND

Craig Childs

SASQUATCH BOOKS
SEATTLE

BLOOMFIELD TOWNSHIP PUBLIC LIBRARY
1099 Lone Pine Road
Bloomfield Hills, Michigan 48302-2410

FOR REGAN CHOI,

A WOMAN OF INEXTINGUISHABLE GRACE

AND STURDY WALKING SHOES

Copyright ©2002 by Craig Childs
All rights reserved. No portion of this book may be reproduced
or utilized in any form, or by any electronic, mechanical, or other means
without the prior written permission of the publisher.

Printed in the United States of America
Published by Sasquatch Books
Distributed by Publishers Group West
09 08 07 06 05 04 03 02   6 5 4 3 2 1

Cover design: Kate Basart
Interior design: Jenny Wilkson
Cover photograph: JD Marston
Interior illustrations and photographs: Craig Childs and Regan Choi
Copy editor: Don Graydon
Photographs: Page viii: Walking a canyon. Page 14: Skull of a child. Page 36: Apache water basket.
Page 70: Bringing the packs down. Page 104: Narrow passage. Page 130: An Anasazi vessel.
Page 146: Island interior. Page 174: Crossing a high ridge. Page 198: Patayan pottery.
Page 216: The dune sea.

Library of Congress Cataloging in Publication Data
Childs, Craig Leland.
Soul of nowhere : traversing grace in a rugged land / Craig Childs.
p.   cm.
Includes bibliographical references.
ISBN 1-57061-306-0 (alk. paper)
1. Indians of North America—Southwest, New—Antiquities. 2. Indians of
Mexico—Antiquities. 3. Southwest, New—Description and travel. 4. Mexico—
Description and travel. I. Title.
E78.S7 C46 2002
979—dc21   2002021721

Sasquatch Books / 615 Second Avenue / Seattle, Washington 98104 / (206)467-4300
www.sasquatchbooks.com / books@sasquatchbooks.com

Contents

Author's Note vi

PROLOGUE—THE LAND 1

CHASM 15

CANYONS 37

PASSAGE 71

LABYRINTH 105

TOWERS 131

ISLAND 147

CRAGS 175

LAVA 199

EPILOGUE—THE SAND 217

Bibliography 227

Acknowledgments 230

About the Author 232

NOV 04 2002

Author's Note

For reasons of preservation, I have left references to specific locations of archaeological sites and wilderness regions in this book as obscure as possible. When geographic names are used, they will not locate a site within an area any smaller than one hundred square miles.

No artifact discussed here was removed from its original location. This was done both for the sake of archaeological integrity and out of regard for the items themselves. If an artifact was moved at all, it was returned to its original position so as not to disturb its context.

A number of photographs and sketches are included in this book. All images, except for two, were taken or drawn by me at the sites; those in the Prologue and the Passage chapter were photographed by Regan Choi.

It rolls and thunders and resounds with warcries
and the penetrating sound of wrathful mantras.
Do not be afraid of it, do not escape,
do not fear.

—The Tibetan Book of the Dead

One further freedom, turn me please to stone.

—José Knighton

PROLOGUE

The Land

I am the man sitting naked in the desert. My hands are clasped at my ankles, knees drawn to my chest to make my body small and simple. A flash of lightning sparks from a thunderstorm miles off. I breathe and listen. No thunder. Below me, around me, cliffs and canyons swim in a litany of moonlight and shadow.

More lightning comes. The rising head of the storm is illuminated from within, a firecracker snap of white. Then darkness.

The day's heat swells from rock faces below, coming up in waves, rolling over me before spreading into the night sky. Something cool touches my shoulder, brief, a wisp of air no heavier than passing silk. I turn my head, expecting to see something. I see the sharp teeth of rock where cliffs have caved in; I see moonlight banding across butte walls; I see in the distance the cauliflower swell of this approaching thunderhead.

Everything is magnified in this land of giants. The faceted cliffs are prisms exaggerating the slightest touch of wind, amplifying the heat, the dryness, and my slow, even breathing. My senses strain just to sit here. Everything leans inward, as if at the edge of a black hole. Rocks and cliffs bend until breaking. The moonlight drifts toward the bottom. My eyes trace thousands of feet down to where shadows gather, where the great walls of canyons come together. The questions never leave my tongue. What is this desolate lure that I feel around me, as sharp and enticing as freshly broken glass?

My clothes lie in a snakeskin pile behind me, out of reach. The shirt is the same one I have been wearing for months now, the only one I have with me. During the day it is my protection from the sun. At night, sitting in the dwindling heat of summer, I get rid of it and every-thing else: my boots with their balding rubber soles, and the binocu-lars that hang all day from a thin, black cord around my neck. And my notebook, too, I leave it with the rest of my things. It is good to be free of them. They have been with me for four months through a province of canyons in northern Arizona, and although they are the very items that keep me sane and alive, I have often thought about launching them off one of these edges, listening with decisive, anxious pleasure to the crash of gear—my hay bale of a pack tearing open and spilling itself, climbing rope thudding like a sack of flour, my metal cup chiming against rocks until I can no longer hear it.

What is down there is a voice, a lure, a landscape alive in its winding shapes, in the light that falls inside and never gets out. I uncurl my body from above it and slowly stand. I walk to my clothes pile to slip on my pants. They are made of light canvas. The knife and its sheath hang loosely from my unbuckled belt. I move slowly. Blued shadows weep across my shoulders. I pull up the belt and buckle it, standing at the edge for a moment. With their distorted moonlit shapes, the landforms all around look like throngs of ghosts. I see faces huge as skyscrapers. It creaks with longing, opening itself: an invitation.

I go barefoot from there, gingerly walking along a platform of rock, leaving my shirt, boots, and gear behind. Numerous canyons and clefts drop beneath me, many of them inaccessible. I cut back around their dark heads, glancing down as I pass, seeing within each a black seam that the moonlight cannot reach. Some canyons send up boils of hot air, while others are completely still, cool even. Crickets sound from below, the pacifying tone of cello strings touched with a bow, hundreds of crickets, and I know that there is water down there, hanging gardens of ferns and dripping seeps in a place where nothing else grows. These canyons are tempting. But I am going somewhere. There is one canyon up ahead.

I glide into it, descending ladder rungs of handholds to a ledge that wraps in and out of the moonlight. Downward stairwells of sandstone are blocked by large portions of fallen cliff and I climb over the debris, my feet tender on the sharpness.

The thunderhead lifts, coming closer, and a hot wind draws up to meet it, coiling through its clouds, forcing lightning out of its folds. I can hear the thunder now. The wind darts around me, a scared school of fish. I recognize the feel of this air. The storm is coming.

There is a cave below here, where I am heading. It is a deep cup within ledges and cliffs. I found it yesterday. I had been looking for a spot to set camp, my pack dragging at my body like a tired child. I ducked into the shelter and after scanning the floor, glanced up to the ceiling. A breath escaped my mouth with a strange sound.

Paintings in numerous colors curved over my head. Paint on top of paint, figures within figures. I lifted my hand uselessly in front of my face, fingers spread as if pushing the wall away from my eyes.

I had heard of this place from another traveler, who told of an unmistakable gallery of apparitions in the desert, but I hadn't known exactly where it was, not any closer than twenty or thirty miles of here. To come across it unprepared was alarming. Heads and eyes had swarmed over me when I looked up. Figures painted in blue, red, ochre, and green stretched across the ceiling above my outstretched hand, their shoulders pinched together like too many genies housed in too small a bottle. Within some, painted organs were visible: hearts, intestines, veins, ovaries. But the bodies looked only vaguely human, more like anatomical diagrams of phantoms. Some had red stigmata circles painted into their open hands. Their torsos bent and spread, becoming alive, as if pulling themselves out of the rock, opening their mouths in the air. Inside of these bodies were images of animals, geometric shapes, and untellable stories played out in multiple colors. Stories within stories.

I knew immediately from the colors and types of figures that the paintings dated back at least three thousand years. The style was a kind used by nomads, desert hunters who once covered about thirty thousand square miles of canyon country. They had come to paint at this blistering edge of the planet.

Why here? Why not on the bison-studded Great Plains, the Pacific Coast with its fish and blackberries, or the sloped and watered foothills of the Rocky Mountains? Why not even forty miles to my back on a mesa top shielded by piñon and juniper trees? They had chosen a different kind of country, one defined by severity. They found some raw element of human longing out here, and it, like everything else, was intensely magnified for them.

Archaeologists call them the Desert Culture, and the ones that came after them they call the Mogollon, the Anasazi, the Hohokam, and the Salado. I don't know what name I should use. The Painters, maybe. Their remains are scattered throughout this landscape, their finely worked stone tools and pieces of basketry left exactly where their hands last let go of them. They tell me that there is a way to live here, that I am not the first or the last, and I am not alone.

This place is more portentous, more enigmatic, than most of the artifact sites I find. I would have set my camp nearer to it, but the thought of sleeping there made me nervous. The cave's figures are weirdly vivid and enticing, as if the strangeness and roughness of this country had a hand in their art.

Even the aboriginal Anasazi who encountered the site a thousand years ago were strangers to it. Archaeologists who came upon it in the 1980s decided that it might once have been a place of shamans. I spoke with one of these archaeologists. When I mentioned the site to her, I saw her change from a federal, managerial scientist to a woman of flesh and imagination. She set her papers down on her desk. She said that archaeology is a science. Artifacts can be categorized, but this place is a different matter, she said, perhaps a vision into a more complete world, maybe a way of understanding this maddening landscape. She told me that she had gone to document the site and that the wind picked up whenever she used her video recorder. She said the wind died each time she lowered the machine.

The wind gathers tonight as I descend toward the cave. The storm is almost here, its lightning sharp. The thunder is a bag of stones given a hard shaking. I smell rain. Not a long rain like that of winter in this part of the world, but a quick and savage rain, the kind that comes to the desert in the late summer. When I look behind me, I see a single fan of clouds huge and spreading, going through dark, dramatic motions of disgorging, reaching down and colliding with the ground. I move swiftly, my bare feet as alert as a slapped cheek. Every tiny pebble. A stick. A warm belt of sand rippled by an old wind.

I am within an interior canyon now, looping the back ledges of its small feeder canyons. I remember the moves I made yesterday, certain crags used to cross the drops, and the trunk of a dead juniper fallen into a crevice, useful as a solid platform, leaping off of it to a ledge. Going into this country is like cutting open a fish. Beneath sleek skin is a place of surprising, visceral oddities, an earthen *Gray's Anatomy*. There are layers within layers, a few familiar shapes but mostly a mystery of bloody fans and tubes, all of it fully functional, spare and essential, but unknown. I climb through these organs, my hands gripping bones of sandstone, fingers hunting for holds the size of ribs.

The spreading roof of the storm blocks the moonlight, sending me into sudden darkness. Rain strengthens its smell, pushing at the wind. The lightning is close, brash white cracks that kick like horses. Lightning touches ground on one of the canyon rims far above me. The sky sears with thunder. I can hear the rain, sheets of water bracing into canyon walls as the storm comes over the edge. There is no rain down here yet.

It is difficult to see where I'm walking now. My feet find the way, lifted high enough with each step so that I don't stub my toes. The wind comes from my right shoulder, overturning small rocks. I want to run to get down to the room of paintings, but I'll wait for the rain to push me. I glance back again and see moonlight swirling into the rain. The day's heat is still rising out of the canyons, twisting the cold rain into misting, urgent spirals. I pick up speed. My eyes pluck gradations of gray from my path, distinguishing angles of rock for the next step. A cactus spine dives into the softness of my arch. I break it off by dragging my sole over the ground without slowing.

The rain arrives. Piercing drops. It sounds like a bellowing machine, water caught up in wind, gears screeching. I run. Everything moves fast, lightning charging through the sky ahead of me, striking ground far below, instantly illuminating a heap of boulders and three craggy juniper trees, then going black. The water begins to run. Mud and sticks set into motion. They pour over edges of rock; my feet splash through, mud spraying against my calves. Rainwater grumbles into holes of foam and uprooted plants. Waterfalls form. The land is suddenly threaded by water, flashing to life. Water comes from everywhere at once, leading down, rushing toward the floor of the canyon, joining and joining.

I duck into the dark eye of an overhang, just big enough to be called a cave. It is dry in here. My hands spread on my thighs. I bend down so that water can drain from my hair. Thin waterfalls start across the face of the shelter and I look up to watch them. They form a dark, sheeting wall, spattering against the solid stone ground with high-pitched tones.

Behind me and above me within this shelter are the paintings. They are well protected from the rain. I had planned on viewing them in moonlight, but in the dark of the storm I see nothing. Every other sense is full, though. I smell everything dead that has been waiting to rot, waiting for the storm to come and bring rain. The air roars with wind and water. I squint over my shoulder, but cannot see even the faintest outline of the paintings. Adrenaline drips cold into my blood, not from the storm, but from the darkness. They can see me but I can't see them.

I crouch close to the sheet of water, my back to the artwork. A match from my pocket could illuminate the ceiling so I might view the paintings, but the moon will return soon enough. Summer storms are full of fanfare and agony, but they are quick. And my matches are probably soaked. I stare at nothing through the sheets of water.

Among the jumble of exotic characters behind me is a single deer painted in black. I remember it clearly because it is the most concrete figure of them all. It has antlers and cloven hooves. Its external anatomy is accurate. Made with very few strokes, it had reminded me of a Japanese silk painting, and yesterday as I studied it, I saw bold, easy gestures used in its creation—strokes made from the shoulder and not the hand, the brush not lifting from the rock until the painting was finished. I had stood in front of it in the last light, clinging to its certainty, while around it floated the hallucinogenic, multicolored shapes of humans turning into animals, of ungodly and beautiful creatures.

I cannot shake this idea that the land painted these images, soaking into the lives of the people who came here. The paintings are an older version of the modern maps that I keep in my gear, a person's judgment of what is critical in this landscape. Only, the maps I carry were compiled by machinery and by people who likely never set foot in this territory, while this artwork is the result of humans commingling with this place. Myself, crouched in this cave, I am hoping to become the same, a person who is changed by the land, who puts a pen to paper and tells what I have seen of this land.

For seven years now I have been traveling the southwestern wilderness, coming out to places that open my life like a knife slipping the seam of an envelope. I have walked bladed peaks rising out of dunes in northwest Mexico; scribbles of red canyons in southern Utah; a sand and gravel wash in the Sonoran Desert as dry as a basket of beans, where coyotes and feral burros come to dig for water; chasms in the border country of Mexico, where the only place to travel is through dark, crooked causeways between boulders. In these seven years, I have had no residence nor telephone number. I have been a pilgrim of erosion, seeking the places that fall away, places of sand and corroding monuments.

Everything is in motion here, the artwork wearing away in dry flakes of paint, boulders unearthed and fallen, always revealing beneath even greater, more alluring terrain. The ground tears open as if reaching for an endpoint, maybe a living mind within, or maybe the emptiness of a peeled onion. I am here because this beast, this rolling, pitching landscape, whispers into the air, and I crouch here, holding my ear next to its mouth, listening.

After a while, the storm moves on to spill into some other canyon. Electricity leaves the air. The thinning barrier of water before me winds into slowing strands. Moonlight comes through here and there, beams landing to illustrate a patch of cliff, a far rim, the canyon floor. The wind is done, and the thunder sounds as if it has been put away in a closet. There is only the mumble of draining water.

The rear of the storm opens and the moon comes into the floor of the canyon, moving downstream. I watch its liquid advance. It seems too liquid, though. It doesn't look like moonlight anymore. It looks like a huge ghost surveying the bottom of the canyon, pausing in places, then gliding ahead, filling the sandy corridor. I try to get a better focus, scooting forward so I can see straight down. The ghost, incandescent in fresh moonlight, sends arms ahead of it the way a blindfolded person would walk through a forest. I don't know what I am seeing.

Wait. There really is something down there. Looking from the very edge, I can see it, clear as if it were a banner blowing along the canyon floor, puffing up, then folding as it rolls. I can see where it bends on itself, dimpled and shaded from the moonlight. Whatever it is, it is real.

I hunt through my mind for reasons and explanations. What had the archaeologist said? There is rational science and then there is this place. There is something inside of this rugged land that is animate, that breathes. I prepare myself. It makes a rising sound. A grinding. A suck and a gulp. Rocks hit each other and are muffled. I hear a groan. Something breaking. Wood.

The sound becomes familiar. Next I smell it, and that too is familiar. It is the musty scent of death, the unmistakable smell of a flash flood. The thunderhead had been enough to begin a deluge in the canyon floor. Parts of upstream trees are broken at their bases, sent down in the water. The front of the flood moves in concert with the moonlight. The customary red of its mud and crushed rocks has been bleached white by the moon. At every crook of the canyon the flood swirls and turns until it is directly beneath me.

At that moment, the moon reaches my alcove. A door opens. Light rushes through, covering my shoulders, covering the ground, the canyon, everything. The light, fine as talcum powder, reflects up from the ground to my chest. My body glows, wet from the rain. Water drips out of my hair.

The light reminds me of why I slipped into shelter here. I turn my head to look over my shoulder. In soft light a gallery of shamans rises over me. My eyes drift across the rows of figures, their bodies stitched with stories, dashes and blocks of color, shoulders and heads and eyes radiant with geometry. Even the simple deer that I had fastened to yesterday, I now see that its body is left purposely hollow, as if within the animal there is something that evades the eye, something beyond simple perceptions. The paint glows. I am made suddenly illiterate. For just these few seconds my mind is as silent as a house at night.

I gradually trace from one painted figure to the next, on down the line as if reviewing a solemn and decorated troop. They stand absolutely silent, while reddish birds, sunbursts, and snakes hover around them. Thousands of years enter my bloodstream. The wind invades my eyes.

Another layer has peeled back. These last seven years I have walked thousands of miles and only now can I feel the earth opening beneath me. I have been traveling this far to see what I am seeing tonight. The canyon spreads, drawing down the flood, pulling in moonlight, and I am picked up, pushed and tumbled, speed increasing, the canyon and its drumming flood boulders pulling me toward the center. This land is made of constant change, every piece of it eroding, and I am becoming part of it, caught up in the movement. My body is tight as a wire, my skin cold, my breath burning. If I move, if I stand, I will shatter.

In desolation we expect to find utter emptiness. There should be nothing but the barren end of the world here, but instead I find an inalienable, voracious presence. The place is alive with its floods, its cliffs, and its silences. These years have brought me closer to this living creature and tonight I am right up against it, the heat of its body pressing on me. Of course I want to go farther. I want to reach into this animal, however many seasons and long treks it will take. I want to see through its eyes.

Fear has stopped me here before. I have feared that if I go too far I will myself erode into nothing after losing my precious supplies of food and water, dying under the sun. And I have also feared that I will live, but will be left unable to speak, my mind handed over to this ineffable vastness.

Tonight the fear shakes off. Perhaps it is called faith. I am soothed and driven by the alignments around me—my body in this alcove at the same moment as the flood passes beneath painted heads, while moonlight strikes through, the wind pushing on my skin, shoving me down here, blasts of lightning and thunder driving into my heart, the weight of a thunderhead passing away, ledges and rubble heaps of cliff walls scraping my feet and showing the way in, years of thirst, waiting through winters as cold as the moon. Every course has led to this inner vault of canyons, to this jagged place where I feel the thrumming heartbeat of the land.

I look across the paintings overhead. Their designs tell how it was once done here, how the world was once perceived. If I follow the people who lived on these verges, if I anchor myself to their generations of knowledge, then I have a chance. I can use them like a rope, a handline on a cliff, as I reach out to share the marrow of the land. I extend my hand toward the ceiling, tracing shapes in the air, pressing these images into my memory.

When I am done, I slowly turn away from the paintings and look out at the canyon, its floor pulsing in flood. The land opens into moonlight. It says *come*.

CHASM

Foot of the Sierra Madre Occidental, Northern Mexico

One beam of sunlight. That was all, leaving everything else in emerald shades of dark. This single shaft fell between the chasm walls, dropping through a gap in a high canopy of maples thick as clouds, then through briars of vines, oaks, and long-needled pines, planting itself on the floor a hundred feet below me. I stood atop masses of crumbled, fallen cliffs, boulders two stories tall, four stories tall. Trees grew up through their clefts, embracing rock faces with elbows and arms of roots.

This viscera of northern, almost tropical forest obscured most of the land around me. What I could not see was the rising outline of this chasm, an enormous rift within the earth. At its widest, its blocky, bare-stone rims are nearly a mile apart. The floor is maybe fifteen, twenty yards wide, cut into the flanks of the Sierra Madre Occidental of northern Mexico. There are other chasms around this one, fields of them opening through the foothills, some hundreds of miles long, splitting the desert below into massive gulfs. From inside, I stood mostly ignorant of this outer world.

I wore long pants and a long-sleeved shirt, a broad-brimmed oilskin hat, and a small pack strapped across my back holding a quart of water, some food, a sketchbook, and a few other necessities. I was a tight bundle of gear and quiet anticipation, studying the course in front of me, how to get down to the sunlight. A gap between boulders presented itself. The passage smelled of moldy bread and mushrooms. I climbed in.

Everything I touched was heavy with information. I pulled free a divot of club moss in search of a handhold, fingers testing the texture, dampness, and shape of the rock, hunting for a knick or a lip. Then below that, a wedged piece of wood to lower myself off of, then a hanging root that I tested for half a second before giving it my full weight. I slid along my boot tips five feet down a chute, catching on a ledge. My body flushed with racial memory, recalling an old way of covering ground, the candid alertness of a primate traveling the rain forest canopy two hundred feet up, grip to grip, bending out on flexible branches to link arms with whatever comes next. There were no manicured routes here, no sidewalks or hallways engineered for my body. I had to re-form myself to fit the place, judging every motion, my mind taut.

No one has lived here for hundreds of years, and even the solitary ranchers who work this region stay out of the chasms. Cliffs stack on each other thousands of feet deep, leaving only narrow walks of flat ground up high and forested swaths in the floors. Up there is a desert of light, a hard, windblasted country as barren as tundra. Down here is a different universe, a gathering place where migrating neotropical birds announce their presence with exotic, watery voices. This is the deep snare into which everything falls, building a chaotic, tumble-down terrain.

It is not possible for me to walk here in the way that I have been taught by my civilization, a place where the feet are blind vehicles. The chasm gives a straightforward set of instructions: go to the bottom and there you will be shown how to move, how to tinker, how to glide, and how to pause. There will be no need for long-distance route finding, no options for climbing out. You will learn inch by inch, using your hands, your ears, your tongue, and the pads of your fingers. You will walk on many levels.

After ten minutes of climbing I reached the horizon of the sunlight. My rhythm changed as I moved toward it over crooks of fallen branches and brambles of vines. I stepped up to a circle of light about two feet wide. I could have reached into it and watched my hand turn an incandescent white, but instead I stared at it, hesitant to touch this strange apparition. I looked up, finding the trapdoor in the canopy where the light originated, a hole where one of these ancient maples had fallen. Through the hole I saw giant stone faces sailing upward, blocking nearly all of the sky.

I skirted the edges of the beam of light, the only straight line to be found anywhere. I don't much care for straight lines. Too lacking in possibility. I knew what would happen if I stepped into it. My body would turn a phantasmal hue, my clothes and skin becoming radiant with bleached light, my shoulders warming instantly. Around me were knots of rotting stumps in the shade, and a floor cushioned by big-tooth maple leaves, many as large as my hand. Poison ivy grew in thickets of upward reaching tentacles. Roots fed across the ground, weaving themselves into mats and triplines. This place was hungry, pulling in everything it could, filling itself with the tumult of the earth. I could smell it all around, the feral, seductive scent of decay and sprouting seeds.

And this solitary ray of sunlight. It was a stranger down here, a thing of logic and propriety fallen into the filthy underworld. I was tempted to at least reach my hand into it, but decided not to. I had only come to look at it out of curiosity. I left it alone. I turned and worked my way deeper into the chasm's throat.

We had not expected this place, these riches. Coming across the desert of northern Mexico, my traveling companions and I had planned on only parched canyons and at the most, waist-high jungles of cat claw bushes. That is all that can be seen from the last paved road. Translucent pillars of dust devils shiver across the plains. There are sand plots of dead agricultural fields and sparse settlements of mesquite trees; an abandoned, roofless adobe house now and then, or maybe a cluster of tar-paper buildings barely holding against the wind, men sitting in their shade. We had found our way past the paved road, out a four-wheel-drive track, and finally to the edge of this chasm on foot, looking thousands of feet down into a nest of trees and cliffs.

I had come with a small team of people performing archaeological research, its members loaded down with articles and reports, scribbling daily academic data into field books. Among them was my wife, Regan Choi, who came with her paints and brushes and sheets of watercolor paper to record the finds. We were hauling our belongings for a month through the barrancas at the outskirts of the Sierra Madre, looking for the remains of a cliff-dwelling culture that had last been here six hundred years ago. Even though we were indeed finding numerous pristine artifacts and multistory dwellings of stone and adobe, we knew that our most remarkable discovery was this place.

When we first climbed into here a couple weeks ago, each of us shouldering a heavy pack, we realized that we had passed into a different kind of country, one that stood our senses on end. We had found a tone of silence and light that altered the way we moved and how we rested, giving weight and slowness to each of our gestures. We walked between great stone walls dizzying in their height, into corridors of vine-wrapped maples and walnuts. In the bottom, a small stream coiled around us, flowing within the topple of boulders, filling the space with the mumble and chirp of water. We had looked at each other in those first hours of travel down here, but we said nothing. Our eyes asked the same question: What is this thing that we have found?

We had arranged to walk here in order to survey this quadrant of an unnamed pre-Columbian culture, but we each knew our true reasons. We were here because we were curious, as all wild things are—curious to feel ourselves change, our bodies stretching and conforming until we were no longer the people we had once been. We wished to become members of a landscape rather than mechanical figures teetering across it.

Weeks of travel brought us boulders and mangy-dark forests, ferns, and unexpected light. I walked back in the early evening dim, returning to the place where the sun shaft had been only hours earlier. It was gone. The light had changed, like fine mist now. And the scent was colder, more like winter stones than the mulch I had smelled earlier. I was moving differently than I had, climbing with greater caution and stopping more often to glance into the hundred shades of darkness surrounding me. Standing where the sunlight had been, the forest looming, I imagined that this must be what every person desires most. Maybe not this place in particular, but this sensation. It is what we mean by immortality. Not to live forever, but to pass into something that does.

It was mostly dark when I arrived back at camp, a pile of gear up high in the cliffs, accessed by a steep, bouldery ravine. Everyone was still out on their daily explorations, so I had the rock shelf to myself. I listened across the distance for the sound of human movement. I heard below me the rustle and flap of birds and winds coming through, but no tromping steps of bipeds.

Camp was on a desert ledge above the roof of the forest, an open view all around. It was like standing on the fortieth floor of a building during a blackout, looking across the shapes of surrounding spires, everything in silhouette. Enormous strikes of cliff faces were falling away, eroded into spindles ready to crumble. All things go to the bottom. Entropy pulls everything back to the nest, to the place where creation lives, down in the forest.

The first person to come was Regan. I heard her steps in the ravine, recognizing something about her, maybe her pace.

"Regan?" I called down. My voice bounced, muffled in the trees and carried off across the cliffs.

She stopped far below me. "Yes."

"Coming home?"

Tired voice, neck craned to see how close she was to camp: "I've got water. Be up there in a minute."

When she started again, I read her route by sound. She came up a ledgy outcrop, climbing slowly with canvas bladders of drinking and cooking water that she had gathered at a spring, one over the shoulder, one in hand—I knew by familiarity of how she wears her gear. I heard her step to an angled tree root, then into the loose rocks above, leading to a path we had left from staying here for a few days. She arrived and let down her load. I could barely see her face, sweetly egg-shaped, the black of her hair tied and fallen over her shoulder to the base of her ribs.

"Good day?" I asked.

In the last light, I saw a smile come across her face. "There are fantastic things out there. Have you seen?"

"Yes," I said. "I've seen some of them."

The next morning I went off with one of the others searching for cliff dwellings, and by early afternoon we had left each other, him heading up one ravine, me up another. The ravines split over and over, steep as ladders, leading to entirely different locations. My ravine finally deposited me on a ledge in open sunlight, eight hundred feet above the forest.

The ledge was clogged with heavy-wood bushes, manzanita and mountain mahogany, not much room for moving. Roots hung over the drop, wrapped around empty space where there used to be pieces of ground. I prodded the tips of my boots in and out of spaces, grabbing firm rock when I could, reaching my arms deep into the bushes for holds. Rocks fell out from under my soles. They turned slowly in the air as they dropped, whistling away. I never heard them hit.

Even in this high, craggy country, along the walls of the chasm we had found signs of ancient people, as if they had once poured over the highest rim, pausing to build balconies of villages on the way down. This morning we had come upon four cliff dwellings recessed into the face, each built sturdily of stone-core walls sealed in adobe, then painted with a fine plaster. Curved portions of broken pots lay on their floors, some brown, others painted in black and orange, some as black and reflective as obsidian. In the largest dwelling, a building of maybe twenty rooms, was a piece of wood carved into a thin disk, used as a whorl for spinning cotton. In a nearby structure six linked spirals painted in black covered the whole of a wall. We took notes and photographs, ducking into the back rooms with our flashlights. It seemed outlandish that they would have built in this slim, tall region, dropping their adobe dwellings into place like losing something down a crack, under the seats in a sofa, the last place you would look. Like us, they had come here. This chasm had always been a gathering place.

High over its floor I moved slowly, aware of every part of my body. The weight of a finger mattered. Perhaps this would have been a good place to use ropes, to make certain that I had a partner nearby, anchored with climbing webbing and mechanical chocks. But my sense of balance was the most reliable protection I could have. Ropes would have shielded me from the face of this chasm, changing my reasons for being here. I left my ledge and climbed between towers broken away, fitting myself into narrow cracks rising to the top. I wanted to go only where my own hands would take me.

The top. It was a platform of rock maybe a quarter-mile wide. The wind came steadily across it, tipping over dry seed-heads of grass left over from the last good rain. I walked with ease now, feet on solid ground. My breath was a different temperature than when I had been climbing, cooler, and slower. Within a couple minutes of walking up here, I realized that I was on an island, a butte carved away from the main rim, cliffs dropping on all sides. I reached its highest point and found a seat on a saucer of volcanic rock, looking into the threading canyons around me, all of them leading down to a single point: a boiling reach of forest far below.

As a child I often imagined jumping from an airplane with a parachute, aiming for the most delirious-looking place, an area that would swallow me. I wanted somewhere that had no roads or cities or towns, a place like this. There I would find engaging remains of ancient civilizations. There would be no possibility for a soft bed or a long, hot shower. I would kill, skin, and eat animals, cooking them on open fires.

In this place that I had imagined, I would walk. Walk with no end.

Walk until I melted into the ground. I stared at the plaster-textured ceiling of my bedroom and imagined the cluttered little shapes to be mountains wall to wall, thousands of miles of wilderness, and me on my way in, floating in my bed as I fell. Perhaps it was a Louis L'Amour brave-explorer fantasy I had, or a *Heart of Darkness* journey that I was after where the severity of my environment would carry me to the edge of my mind, exposing realms beyond admissible vision. I somehow knew as a child that within isolation and ruggedness was a way of accessing the unexpected from the world.

It wasn't heroism or glory that I hoped to find in these places. Rather, it was the odor of rain, it was encountering an animal alone in heavy woods, or the moment in trackless country when I realize that I am utterly lost and suddenly there is no separation between me and the ground beneath me. I imagined an exhaustively physical landscape, like the ones I encountered on hikes with my mother across ice-shredded timberline ridges, or with my father hunting quail in far desert arroyos.

Maybe it is a genetic splinter that I have, one that is necessary for the survival of the species. It says to a certain number of us, *Go.* It says, *Find what is out there, know what is out there, become what is out there,* sending us away as if getting rid of us to perish or plant a seed, or just to never be heard from again. So I went.

Now that I was here, sitting on the high point of this butte, I felt the weight of this place as if the ocean was on top of me. This barranca country of chasms went on to the horizons, gaping into sheer, open plunges all around. The wizardry I experienced here was as astonishing as a magnet taken through a box of nails. Even the most lifeless objects were brought to attention, revealing a purpose, an intent, even an invisible desire. My wits stood straight up, commanded to do so.

My breathing settled from the earlier climb. My eyes adjusted to the openness up here. When I was ready, rested, I walked to a nearby edge, finding a ravine that cut down its side, and began descending. A couple minutes down, fit into the long, narrow mouth of a cave, was a beautiful face of adobe dwellings. Fawn colored, they could easily be passed by, mistaken for solid rock walls except for their dark doorways, and even these could be dismissed with a quick glance, shadows slightly out of place.

I approached the first door, a low T-shaped entry that had been constructed with smooth corners, easy to slip in and out of. I took off my hat and my pack, setting them on the ground out front so that they would not get in my way. As if walking into a shop crowded with china, I wanted to know the exact dimensions of my body, no coat sleeves or loops to catch unexpectedly. I pulled a small, red light from my pocket and entered, making certain that my shoulders did not scrape the doorway.

My steps came slowly as I scanned the ground, the inside of the first room half-lit, its floor strewn with broken pottery and corncobs. Corn was the primary crop here and in the dryness of the ruin the cobs will last thousands more years. I paused at the torn corner of a woven mat, crouching. It was half-buried in debris and dust, its warp and weft barely visible under my light. I had seen a number of partial, woven artifacts in the other ruins here. They had been prolific weavers. How much more was there, beneath the debris? I did not move it.

Then I hunched through the second door, rectangular, into an interior

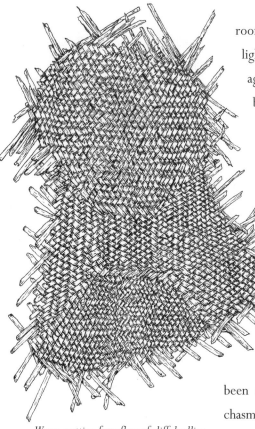

Woven matting from floor of cliff dwelling

room with hardly any natural light at all. This room opened again into a broad hallway between interior buildings, a few rising two stories into domes in the cave's roof. The cave was deeper than I had expected. Rooms went on into the dark. My light passed smoke-black ceilings and heavy, hand-carved beams that had been cut and hauled from the chasm floor. The beams were caked with soot. I placed my hand on one, feeling its sturdiness, and the sharp cut where it had been planed, giving it ninety-degree corners. What was it, seven hundred pounds of solid wood? Brought at least a thousand feet up the butte wall to here. And how many of them? I probed the passage with my light. More than twenty beams were within view, some vertical and posted into adobe collars in the floors, others horizontal overhead. It had taken incredible labor to build a community here. Or maybe not so much labor as finesse. Giant timbers and water for this much adobe had to have been maneuvered up to here with leverage and precision.

Walking along the hallway I imagined that they had found the way to live here. Like an improbable balancing act, there had been a method that made this possible, a mutual understanding with this place. I wondered why we had not found their buildings in the forest, only up in the high caves. Perhaps this was a respite, a place to escape the constant exertion down in the boulders and trees where senses are stretched threadbare at every glance. Of course, the cliffs are defensible fortresses in themselves, a place to hide from enemies and from the darkness of the forests.

I, too, enjoyed the relief of this upper territory, and I thought back to the positioning of our most recent camp, much like this on a high ledge instead of along the forested floor. It was a place to return to after a day of pushing and climbing through the vegetation, a place where we could sit with quiet inoccupation.

I slipped through one of the inward doorways, entering a completely darkened chamber. The only light was a dusty haze floating through a ventilation shaft in one of its walls. Two bats spun around me, panicked by my trespass. They fluttered with the soft sounds of fabric, and dove through the door behind me, escaping. With the motion gone I turned my light to the floor and saw there a single woven sandal. It was a sandal for the left foot. Rodent droppings were stuck to the creases of its weave. Wood rats.

The foot side bore the well-used imprint of its owner. I traced my finger along the shape of this person's stride, asking questions. Here was the heel pressing outward and the gathered bulge just before the ball of the foot. The person had walked with most of the weight toward the outside, rolling the foot along the edge rather than landing flat-footed, as most Americans do now. The person's big toe took very little pressure when stepping off, suggesting that the next foot was already firmly on the ground before body weight shifted. There was no kick-off to the next step. The back foot actually floated off the ground and ahead, no weight to it at all. It was the kind of step you would take when walking through a puddle, trying not to splash, or across a sheet of ice. I move this way while stalking animals or stepping as quietly as possible through dry leaves. It is not a way of walking on city sidewalks, not the step of a person who trusts the ground for its regularity.

I followed the foot pattern with my light, the questions for this person slipping out. Did this land breathe down your neck like it breathes down mine? Did you come in from the open desert and stare at the monumental walls of this chasm? Or were you as indiscriminate and skilled as a worker ant here, this place nothing but a piece of land on which to live?

But how could it have just been a piece of land to you? You had to haul your life into its cracks. It pushed against you. I can see it in the way that you walked. Your body was alert to every step. And how often did you take your sandals and walk down in the chasm floor just to mingle with the deep shades?

The sandal remained silent in response. It rested as it had for the last six hundred years, holding dust, abandoned like everything else here. I turned off my light, seeking quiet. I stopped the questions in my head. The darkness of the ruin and the cave flooded in.

The next day it rained, a hushing rain that leaked through the canopy to the floor of the chasm. I was down here with Regan, walking the lower reaches. She kept her hair tied in a braid that dropped from the back of her hat. She carried her day's supplies in a small pack around her waist, her water slung over a shoulder. Our ways of carrying gear were our own rituals, buckles placed in certain ways, weight shifted to fit our different gaits, a knife or a notebook within quick reach.

We both wore the same dense vegetation on our bodies like a heavy cloak, coming down stairways of colossal boulders. Climbing ahead of me, Regan moved like a monk through the rain. Her body was small in the setting, the round heads of boulders rising far above her, leaning over her, tapestries of moss hanging down. There was nothing swift about her gestures, nothing harried as she lowered herself off the back of a fallen, angled pine, careful not to slip on the swollen lichens. She made minor concessions, finding a handhold in another place, returning to a boulder top to find a new way down.

We said nothing out loud, other than an occasional warning of a dead end or a mess of poison ivy. From thirty feet away I listened to every wrinkle of her clothing and the softness of her boot soles on water-soaked wood. Thunder came through subtly, causing the ground to vibrate as if tympani heads had been barely touched by fingertips. Rainwater dripped down leaves of maple and ash. Regan turned to look up, to let rain land on her face. I saw the faint haze of her breath.

This is a purely sensual landscape, sexual in its shape and its seduction.

Boulders around us were seized by lichens. Drapes of vines unfurled from the canopy, some as thick as my wrist with strings of bark hanging loose. Everything had a texture: the gritty, ruttish scent that came from the ground, and the densely liquid sounds of Regan's passage. Even the light could be touched, a gauze of rich, earthen colors hanging in front of me. No wonder there are global myths of a beautiful, luminous woman who roams the forests, and if your eyes find her, you will follow her out of pure longing and never return. Every story has its basis. This kind of place lures each sense into an inescapable wash of emotion and desire.

I could not remember a moment in my life when I was so impressionable. I had long kept myself distanced just enough from the landscape, escaping when I needed into memories or stories in my head, anything to shelter me from the unremitting persuasion of wilderness. When I had been out for too long alone, or in a landscape too raw and demanding, my being itched with provocation and I had to scratch, finding distraction in a book I had carried along or in doodling for hours with a stick in the sand. To stare directly into the eyes of a place like this, to not look away, is nearly unbearable.

Now I was just beginning to learn how to walk and how to see, how to take in everything around me without panicking or retreating. The multitude of forms in this forest needled through my observations, through my skin, leaving me buzzing with sentience. I began walking on the outer edges of my feet, rolling onto the ball as if throwing pottery with my steps. I studied the ground with my weight, alerting myself to every permutation. I watched Regan, how she moved like water, like darkness, and I imitated her.

I found a nest of bones on a bed of fallen leaves and I called her over. It was an entire skeleton tidily unfolded by a mountain lion, the remains of a white-tailed deer killed and dragged into the clearing. A kill from how long ago? Two weeks? Nine days? We both moved toward it, our hands reaching out to touch the bones as if passing through silk. I imagined that the deer, like the ray of light I had found days earlier, had become trapped down here, caught in the dead ends of boulders and cliffs, suddenly aware of the scent of a mountain lion.

"Taken at the neck," I said, lifting the train of its upper spine, finding the gap where it had been severed from the skull. "A good kill."

Regan nodded. Her hand followed a rib along its arc. "Very neatly done," she said. "I like the way mountain lions kill."

I examined the artful spans and wings of vertebrae. I thought of bones that I have collected, a habit that I ended a few years ago, finally not wanting to remove them from their ground. The teeth of elk, a skull of a mountain lion and a black bear, the pelvis of a rhea, the arm of a raven. I have gathered bags of shells and crab claws, pulling these things out for viewing when I want to stare at the elegant interior of life. I have a fascination for getting to the bottom of things. In the past decade I have traveled with paleontologists, geologists, and archaeologists, taken up residence in libraries to study fluid dynamics or population biology. I have found each of these disciplines to be nothing but lesser forms of osteology, the study of bones, an attempt to get to some central truth. Nothing is hidden by bones.

In certain landscapes, the planet reveals its skeleton. I come here for this reason, walking the bones of the earth. There are no ambiguities other than what I bring with me, and even those begin to wear away in this place. Innumerable times I have sat in the study of skeletons like this, observing methods of the kill, patterns of growth, vectors of decay. It is easy to imagine that when the world and its animals are worn down there will be nothing but a dull emptiness at the center, that bones would be nothing but humble stick figures. But bones are not simple. They are spiraled, hinged, strangely formed, ridged, inter-locked, and artful. They come in fans, rays, and bulbs. They suggest an infinite, powerful order beneath my feet.

I set the top end of the deer's spine exactly back where I found it, trying to hold this lay of objects undisturbed. This is grace, I thought. This is the beautiful woman of the forest that I follow. Death and maple leaves fallen all over each other. The violence of boulders thrown to the floor, and then the creeping consumption of moss and poison ivy. The interior workings of the earth.

Finally we stood from the skeleton and moved on.

Farther ahead we left the floor and climbed to one of the inner benches, entering the steep desert that hangs like a threat over the forest below. We followed the bench to where we found a southeast-facing cliff dwelling, maybe eight single-story rooms in a row. Many of the adobe walls had been painted with black, green, and red images. One was crowded with geometrical human figures and more recent scratchings from Mexican ranchers who had found their way in. One was a crude image of a woman and a man embraced in sex, arms and legs wrapped around each other so that it was difficult to tell where one body began and one ended.

I stepped into back storage rooms, then into the daylight of the front rooms. Beside a tangle of yucca cord on the floor, I saw a dry gourd and picked it up.

I did not drop it when I discovered that it was not a gourd, but a child's skull. Cradled into my palm, the hollow of its eyes swung up toward me. I almost said something out loud, announcing an artifact, but I stopped my voice. I knew it would be strained with excitement, when excitement was not all that I wanted.

The skull belonged to a five- or six-year-old, the nose and eyes and mouth still strangely small against the oversized cranium. The divisions of the skull had yet to fully fuse, allowing the bones to unhinge at several places. The first adult molars had just been in the process of breaking through the gums when the child died. It still had its scalp, and on the scalp were needlepoint pores where there would have been hair.

"There's a skull here," I said quietly, and Regan came through a doorway. Expecting to find it on the ground, she looked up surprised, seeing it in my hands. "I thought it was something else," I told her. "So I picked it up."

She stood in front of me for a while, watching me, looking at the skull in my hands and back to me. I have always been cautious and uncertain around human remains. But it was in my hands now.

It was a light object, no heavier than an emptied coconut. I imagined a child in this landscape. Running along the vegetated floor, not even pausing, in a hurry to get somewhere, maybe taking a message to a dwelling on the opposite side, scrambling through the boulders—the same boulders we had just negotiated to get here. Climbing the crotches and spans of a sycamore tree; aware of mountain lions when alone; learning firsthand not to walk barefoot in poison ivy. I imagined life here, a child testing the parameters of her or his body, learning how to glide to get from one place to the next.

I thought of my own childhood wishes to find a place like this, to move freely and with confidence across the land. But I did not dare compare myself to this child, not at any age. The emotional and personal details of the child's life were utterly inaccessible to me. The only thing I could know about him or her was this terrain, this country that we both traveled.

I saw that Regan was deeply curious. I handed the skull to her. She gingerly took it and sat. She turned it to see every angle, moistening her lips, passing a finger over its brow.

I asked if it troubled her to have a child's head in her hands.

She looked up. She said no. She said that this was a beautiful thing. A child.

I looked at the dusty floor where I had found it. I wondered about the parents. Had the father buried his pain in daily tasks? Had the mother, in a sobering personal ritual, recalled every year that her child would have lived and grown?

I saw people's lives all over this chasm, crying and speaking in casual tones and busy with work. I saw generations upon generations, and this place as familiar as the bedroom, porch, and living room of a house, the place where you grew up, every scent and object well known. Each chasm here was a neighborhood peppered with cliff dwellings, as comfortable as streets and lawns and backyards.

I corrected myself as I watched Regan handle the skull. To have grown up here, I thought, would not have been as simple as living in a suburban house in a well-lit neighborhood. This place is full of sorcery. The company of these entangled woods and their crowning, weather-beaten cliffs overwhelms any dwelling built by human hands. For this child, impregnable wilderness must have been all around, as it was for me now.

Why would they have come here, I wondered. Certainly it could have been to escape warfare, or to build an agricultural community in these well-watered chasms. But while other people lived in cities of the desert plain surrounding the Sierra Madre, these people chose this distant terri-tory. Was it a longing that could not be answered in more gentle coun-try? People don't just live in rigorous terrain because there is nothing better to do. They don't raise children on the face of a chasm on a whim, hauling massive timbers up the cliffs, painting plaster against an adobe wall that sits over the abyss. This landscape has something that they were after, something that I seek to be part of, if for no other reason than to know what it is. This place was the veneer. I wanted to reach down and pull it back, to get underneath it, closer to the bones.

Regan set the skull on the ground, back into the depression where I had first found it. She looked at me for a moment, then turned and smoothly ducked through one of the adobe doorways.

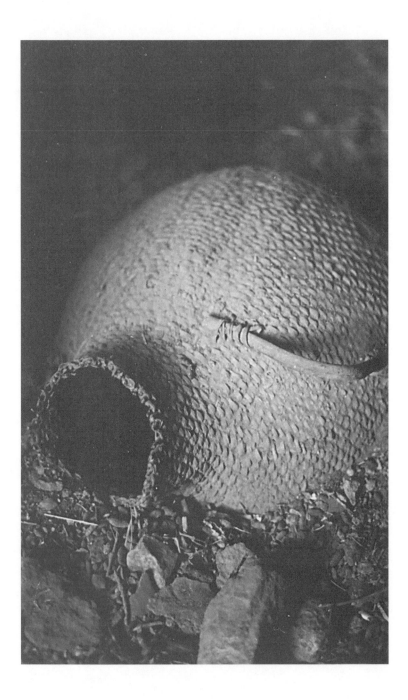

CANYONS

Below the Mogollon Rim, Arizona

A three-hundred-mile-long crest of earth shaves Arizona across its middle, from the end of the Grand Canyon near the Nevada line all the way to New Mexico. For most of its length it is called the Mogollon Rim and it tilts like a boat with a fat man sitting alone in back. The backside, to the north, is a sinking platform that nudges away the barely moistened arms of the Little Colorado River. The southerly front lifts proudly, a frontispiece of stone that rises over central Arizona. Narrow, paper-cut canyons gouge into its face, as if trying to drag it back down, leaving hundreds of miles of long, deep marks.

During my childhood this is the region that saw me most often. I learned to fish at the headwaters of its longer canyons and lived once in a small town where the rim turns to mountains in eastern Arizona. I knew only a limited geography at the time: that there were roads paved with pine needles at the top of the rim, and gravelly desert roads at the bottom. In between was a hundred miles of nowhere, a place vacant of electric lights. I used to look across this territory from up high, or eat my picnic lunch at a canyon head, staring down, wondering what was in there. My mother, a carpenter and traveler, told me that she imagined that there were hordes of raspberries to be picked and places where a person could sit with a canvas and paints and never stand up again. My father, an achingly drunken philosopher who did not live with us, said that there was a wild and grisly truth down there, demons, dangers, and wonderful light, and *snap!* it could swallow you just like that.

What did I believe was down there? A land that would shelter me, where I would never hear neighbor's dogs in the distance, where an airplane across the sky would be cause to stare. A place so unyielding and isolated that I could walk naked if I wanted, assured that not a single person would spy my pale body among the boulders. I believed that there would be canyons, massive hallways of stone as countless as the stars. It was mythical country for me. The very word *canyon* suggested to me protection, a dramatically confined place under the guard of impenetrable cliffs; walls drawn narrowly inward on both sides and the sky a ribbon above. It was a place that would hold me.

I came to this place one winter with Laura Slavik, one of my first and sturdiest traveling companions, the woman who had acted as "best man" in my wedding with Regan Choi. She is one of my urban counterparts . . . living in Denver, Santa Fe, Portland, or Seattle depending on the year. She worked as a waitress, as a journalist, and in women's shelters and with sexually abused children. Whenever possible, we met either in the city or in these lost, rugged landscapes and slipped in as if we belonged there, hoping to be swallowed.

We came this winter in hopes of finding remains of people who had been swallowed before us, their cliff dwellings abandoned, artifacts still lying about as if the people had slipped from the surface, out of view into the interior. This place had been a harbor for numerous cultures, the end point of a fourteenth-century exodus during a time of widespread violence. It was difficult terrain, very little level ground, all cliffs, and canyon floors steep as mountain faces.

We shoved our way out of the dense, high-desert chaparral, wooden batons of branches swatting against our shinbones. We emerged into a clearing midway up a terraced wall, six days into the country on foot. Our breath was visible in the coming evening, ghosts rolling from our mouths. A canyon plunged beneath us, crowded in the floor with oaks and cypress trees and tangles of grapevines. But more than plants, there was rock. Cliffs staggered among each other as if jockeying for position, huge faces as gray as fire ash. They were all crammed above and below us, leading into steel-cold passages where walls closed in until finally touching. In the forested thread that streaked downward, temples of boulders rose above the heads of trees. The trees barely held on in this steepness, clutching the boulders with their roots, leaning over open falls, grabbing onto each other. Everything here is captured, just about to fall, boulders choked into bottlenecks, towers of rock fallen and leaning across to the other side.

Compared to the chasm I had traveled at the edge of the Sierra Madre, this is the eye of a needle. Instead of an enormous, yawning mouth, this territory is filled with dark, innumerable cracks. Each canyon is a quickly drawn breath, something hidden behind the back, tucked out of sight. Each offers a rough and uncommon kind of shelter, one that a simple roof can never provide.

We had been crossing a terrace between canyons for the last four hours, kicking loose rocks and ripping through vegetation, fists locked on branches to pull them apart, searching for our next canyon, our next crack to crawl down into, our next cradle. There had been small drainages along the way, too steep and unformed to call canyons. These were dangerous places where instead of floors there were precipices scraped clean by gravity. We strung across these with our packs, taking half a minute for every step, body weight brought toward the center, hands tight on the rock wall. Now that we had reached the edge of a true canyon, a definite mark on the map, I was relieved. We had found a place to breathe. I looked to Laura, her eyes scanning the depths ahead of us. Even though I could see trepidation in her expression, questions about how we might navigate these drops, she also looked relieved. Instead of being exiled for the night to brambles and open faces, we could call these dark, narrow shafts home. A home like sleeping in a wizard's back room, whispers leaking from the walls.

On a sheer cliff maybe a hundred feet above us and on the opposite side of the canyon was a small cliff dwelling, a simple stone-and-mortar building tucked into a cave. We scanned it with binoculars from our clearing. There was no way to reach it. Agreed, none at all. Around the cliff base were mounds of low, scrubby oaks and shattered boulders. There was no ledge series, no run of handholds leading to it.

This is the land of radical housing, keyholes and perches. I imagined cold nights here centuries ago, residences marked by pinpoints of cliff-dwelling firelight, a place of comfort. On this trip we had already explored a number of multistory dwellings on ledges that I would ordinarily not even consider for sleeping. These people had orchestrated entire villages along slim protuberances. They had built sturdy walls between themselves and some outside threat, their homes and themselves becoming parts of the canyons. They sank themselves into a place huge beyond the capacity of oncoming armies.

From our clearing, Laura gaped up at this ruin, ridiculously far up the cliff. "Monsters," she said. I knew what she meant. They had needed to be safe from monsters, otherwise they never would have built so far up. They had come to the one landscape that could offer sanctuary, and crawled up into its fur, snug against its breast.

I asked her what monsters, but she said again, as if I should know, "Monsters."

The cliff dwellings here likely dated to the fourteenth century and had been built for reasons so far not fully known, constructed by the fringes of a culture called Hohokam, a little bit of Anasazi from the north perhaps, and maybe some Mogollon influence from the east. Customarily, they are called the Salado people, an ethnic conglomeration, a coming together of different cultures under this umbrella of canyons.

Their dwellings may have been hiding places from standing armies in the wealthy, agricultural regions to the southwest where Phoenix now lies. They might have been retreats for raiders in the Sherwood Forest of the Mogollon Rim, or merely convenient ledges upon which to build in this difficult terrain. Or they were the final destination of people driven from their homelands, the only place that they could go expecting asylum, hoisting their refugee villages into the cliffs, the land all around strung with barbed wire canyons.

I imagine that living here, these people found a unique urgency for weather and for how a rock type can influence the day's travels. I believe that they were sharpened to an edge by this place, not allowed to grow self-satisfied or languid.

We set a camp near this inaccessible ruin. It was a ledge camp, a small clearing in the brush with an immediate fall at our feet. After dinner Laura and I sat at the edge. We kept our voices low when we talked so that echoes would not flush the canyon. We heard water far below.

"This ruin back here," she said, gesturing behind and up with her head. "You think there's a way to it?"

I followed her gesture, looking back at the cliff, although all I could see was a black face. "Somewhere," I said.

"That took guts, building up there. I've been desperate and scared before, but I don't think I've been that bad off."

"Maybe they just wanted to sleep well," I said, looking at her.

"A long way to go to sleep."

"I figure they came from someplace else, someplace with monsters, like you said. If you think you're going to wake up every night with a knife at your throat, you're not going to get much sleep, so you go find a safer place." I studied her form, her body slender, her frame rising to broad shoulders and firm muscles like a healthy, possibly dangerous fighter. She was pulled into herself against the cool night, her eyes looking across the canyon as if asking something with half her mind, leaving the other half to talk with me. It is the question that brings sanctuary, I thought. Laura held this nameless question on her tongue, staring. She was hearing the answer as we talked, the canyon pulling on her.

"Still," she said with the half of her mind directed toward me. "That is a lot of work, getting your house moved up into a cliff like that."

"They needed protection," I said.

"From what? Don't you think they could have set up shop right here? This is a perfectly good ledge. You can see anyone coming from above or below."

"I see it more like fully committing yourself."

She wasn't moving. Was she listening to me? Her mouth hung slightly open, as if words were coming out.

"I don't think this is a place to be afraid of," she said, her voice inquisitive, as if she was about to step out on the ground, hoping it was solid. "It feels secure to me. You have to get over the hugeness of it, and all of this goddamned climbing. I think people came here for something other than fear," she said. "I think they came for the same reason you do," her head turning slightly, listening for the sound of water, the sound of emptiness below us. "You want this place to take you in."

I kept quiet to this. I thought about it. Doesn't everyone want this? Isn't this why we string railing at the edges of great and rugged vistas, because people will come from all over the world, flocking right to the lip? If there was nothing to stop them, they would sail off into the abyss. I thought about the Grand Canyon, how every year, damn the railing, four to six people step off and are atomized by the fall. It must be true, I thought. We all want to be absorbed by this place.

"Don't you want this same thing?" I asked.

She had lost herself, looking out there. "Yeah . . . me," she came back, her head sinking so that she could see her body. "I guess we're all here for sanctuary. We all need some sleep." Her voice sounded resigned. She stood, her body unfolding, layers of clothing sounding like a blanket coming out. The way she moved gave signals of finality and fatigue, off to sleep now. She touched my shoulder as she went, a full hand passing over me. "Goodnight."

"Night."

I listened to her get her things out, creating a snug sleeping world for herself, spreading her tarp and her pad, fluffing up her sleeping bag. She cinched her gear sacks, tying knots, getting everything squared away.

Sanctuary. The word stayed with me as I sat on the edge. What kind of sanctuary is this? It is not the simple veneer of a shelter, a place out of the wind. No, in fact it seems to gather wind. It is shelter like the stinging arms of an anemone for a clownfish. The poison becomes part of the animal; the ruggedness becomes the people.

Ten hours later the breakfast was oatmeal with wild grapes and dried hackberries gathered from a nearby tree. Heavy frost on our belongings.

We saw in the first light a three-story ruin nearby. It was so concealed by overlapping rock walls that only a second glance weeded it out. It stood just above our camp in a closeted crevice, filling the space as if it had been poured in, with a black rectangle for an entrance dabbed into place high off the ground.

When we arrived we found the structure standing about twenty-five feet tall, stonework mortared unerringly into a fissure. The rocks used were long, thin table-stones cut to fit. We sat beneath it for some time. To enter the ruin would require care, climbing up the cave wall and sliding over to the doorway. From the ground below we could see inside, up through the single entrance. Multiple levels hid behind the front piece, a congregation of rooms huddled in seclusion. We could see interior hatchways in the ceilings and a single ladder still in place.

We climbed inside. Distracted sunlight roamed from rock to rock, turning mostly to shadow. Spiderwebs clung to the fire-blackened timbers. Ceilings hung just high enough for us to stand. I came up through the hatchway to the second floor and at eye level saw wooden beams crossed with flagstones, then mortared and repeated so that the ceiling was more than a foot thick. They had built with extraordinary care.

I stood on this next level, the wooden ladder beside me, propped through the hatchway to the next level again. I touched it. The wood was oiled by skin, smooth like the inside of an abalone shell. Laura had already gone ahead, walking along the third story. I let her go from my senses, running my hand on the slickness of ladder wood.

"This ladder," I said quietly.

"I know," she responded, her voice far off.

I looked up but could not see her.

The ladder was too weak, or at least too valuable, to use for reaching the third level. I climbed the parent rock of the cave up to the hatchway, just as Laura had done before me. When I crawled up and stood on the third floor, Laura was gone. Where? I strapped on a headlamp and walked into the dark of the rock crevice looking for her.

A wall had been built back here, smoothly mortared, crossing the span in front of me with a low door offset slightly to the left. Two wooden poles leaned against the wall, material for another ladder. This dwelling, I realized, had been constructed in much the same way as the canyons. They were both tightly packaged inside of a much larger, overpowering environment, built tall and narrow, with slender passageways and shielded interiors. I was being led by the shape of architecture, sent from one room and level to the next, following a ladder, a passage, a doorway.

This was an apartment of stairwells, its floors steeply linked— much like the levels of this canyon—with places to sleep and rest, and places to climb. I wondered if this had been the only way to build here, by mimicry. I have seen this same phenomenon in many settings: the tipis of forest edges in Colorado and Wyoming, the broad, simple yurts of high and arid plateaus, butte-top pueblos with their block architecture, and clustered metropolitan skyscrapers standing in cities of both plains and coasts as if answering the smoothness around them. It is this style of canyon architecture that in particular draws my attention.

*Ladder coming through to top
floor of a Salado cliff dwelling*

These Salado cliff dwellings are inseparable from the cliffs that they inhabit, as blended and fine-tuned as a brown moth on tree bark.

Pausing in this dwelling, I understood that I was at the meeting point where land and human graft into each other. This is where people were formed by the canyons, driven by their severity and sheerness to build spindles of dwellings in the rock. The land here changes us into its own shape, covering us. The very mechanics of my eyes and my way of seeing were being re-formed as I traveled, wanting to sleep only in the canyons, induced to climb up into its cracks and hunker there. I was being taken in, as had the people before me.

I entered the next chamber. Still, I did not see Laura. She's been absorbed, I thought. I could, in fact, imagine her stepping into this darkness and completely unveiling herself to it, vanishing. Was she here? I swept my light around, looking for her shape in the rock walls.

The passage deepened into a cavern, losing the trappings of mortar and carved stones. I began to see a dull blue glow ahead. I followed this, turning as the cave crooked to my left. This new light became brighter. Sunlight. I switched off my light as it lost its effect. I emerged into a room that opened to outside air, a lofted ceiling glowing with a backlighting of sun. Laura's body stood outlined in direct sunlight, and in front of her was the opening of the first ruin, the unapproachable stone-and-mortar wall we had seen yesterday. The passage had led through the core of the cliff to come out here.

Standing with her back completely shadowed, Laura did not move. I came beside her. She was looking out of the ruin, standing on a balcony that dropped down the face. The alignment of this natural opening gave a view of maybe forty miles, a telescope pointing out of the canyon. The land out there rolled like a bad sea.

Why would they have assembled this room and its parapet here? I could see no function, except perhaps for framing the view, forming a window for a security lookout. The room had been built to lead its occupant to the edge where I now stood at a stone railing beside Laura. The terrain visible from here was daunting and invulnerable, and it was clear from our view that we were pleated deep inside of it. Could they have built for this reason, for this visual sensation? I let my gaze rove around the engineered enclosure, pausing on its details, low steps of walls to my back, and squared-off blocks of rock set into a liberal padding of mortar.

Everything here brought me to this opening, this view making an announcement: You are now fully recessed into the land. You are inside now. It is time to change and become a person of this place. Most likely it was, indeed, a defensive observatory. Still, I imagine sentries standing here lost in this visual comfort of isolation, believing themselves as impenetrable as the land around them.

When I looked beside me, Laura was consumed, as if staring into the center of a spiral. Without looking at me, she asked, "You see why they came?"

A little less than a year after that hike Laura contacted me. She needed sanctuary again. Her voice quaked. I told her I would make arrangements as quickly as possible. She came in November from the city—

Portland, Oregon. The night before she left, a woman attempted suicide in the battered women's shelter that she helped manage. The woman had slashed her wrists and was immediately hauled off in an ambulance. Laura was left to clean the bloodied bedside table and the sheets strewn as if a storm had come through.

As soon as the mess was squared away, she quit her job, let her apartment go, and drove to Arizona. She needed to be taken back in by the canyons. We arranged with Colin Wann, a close friend of mine who had just graduated from high school, to enter a region below the Mogollon Rim on foot. Laura arrived to meet us. She had urgency in her eyes, her gear packed and ready. We parked on a fire road in the pines and hauled our equipment like creeping animals into the canyons below. We would return to the vehicle in exactly one month.

The second day out she skidded and scratched down a boulder field, landing on her side. Her arms, legs, and back were badly scraped, her pack hanging lopsided from her body, wanting to drag her even farther down. With great effort she sat herself up, dragging her hands off of her damaged skin. She rubbed the blood between her fingers, pleased and mesmerized with it. She lifted a hand to show us, as if in victory, that it was her own blood.

Bolts of canyon walls stagger upward, two thousand feet, three thousand feet, barely adhering to the earth. The igneous rock breaks in a way that leaves ninety-degree-angled joints of sharp, dark lines along countless isometric blocks. These crimp into black cavities, damp and cool. Late on November days an apricot glow comes out of these fissures from low, reflected angles of sunlight. It is into this complex, busted land with its areas of secret light that we traveled.

In general, there was not much talking in this group of three. Colin, whose body was taut and teenage, his muscles snakelike, had the behavior of a young monk. Each night, as we sat around a small fire or around nothing, suddenly he would be gone, simply missing, not to be seen again until morning. He practiced stalking us, waiting in dry leaves and boulders, and slept in places where he could not be found.

Laura had a crucial quietness around her, less experimental and lighthearted than Colin's. This year there was an imperative in the way she approached the land. Colin and I were like tangling monkeys, clamoring in the rocks, while she carried a graveness, the harried look that young mothers often have, cutting to the chase. Whatever had happened in the city, it nearly broke her. It made her eyes sharp and hungry. Daily she moved forward, looking for something that I could not see, sorting among the boulders as if this thing was lost here, somewhere just ahead.

In the wilderness, Laura seemed more raw than when I saw her in the city. Her doors were open here, her skin scraped into scabs and blood streaks. Her face was smudged. She had made an arrangement with this landscape, unveiling herself in front of it instead of hiding. You can hide in the city, I think, but not here. Here, you are suddenly under the constant glare of this landscape. Laura had accepted this. Many times I had seen her naked in the backcountry, standing boldly atop boulders, her body trim and bruised from the journey.

Up in the shadowed pitches where we walked were beautiful, isth-mian forests. Water ran miraculously from somewhere up higher, pouring through fern groves, loud through dances of boulders, send-ing narrow, white waterfalls down rock faces. On the eighth day Colin, Laura, and I sat quietly against our packs, resting in our travel from canyon to canyon. We had a topographic map across the ground. It was haywire with contour lines, no sense in trying to figure anything out from it.

A brief wind came through, tunneling down the canyon, plucking autumn sycamore leaves from overhead and letting them loose. We sat as they fell around us, our necks craned to watch. Each fell differently, obeying the unaccountable providence of wind and the designs of growth. Some pirouetted in theatrical dives, while others rotated slowly, dipping through branches, meandering to the ground. They sounded like pages of newspaper landing.

Laura began to applaud. While she clapped, arms lifted, I looked around me, watching the leaves fall like slow shooting stars dwindling their way to the ground. This could not be an act just for her. No, I told myself that these canyons are filled with random performances, leaves falling with every breeze. Never in my studies of natural history or in my curiosity about my surroundings had I believed that the land was a creature of decisions. Alive, yes, by certain definitions. Breathing with wind, and moving over the millions of years the way a vine creeps across the ground, searching. But in my mind, the land was never a thoughtful animal. It was always stone, solid and unaware.

Still, I could not help but imagine that this moment was strictly between Laura and the canyon, and the canyon somehow knew that she was here.

We moved up this drainage. As it tapered, the walls grew taller. Moss and ferns gathered in the floor. We followed paths of waterfalls. Cascades doubled back on themselves between boulders, splitting, rejoining, and filling deep holes. We reached for each other, pulling up hands and packs. The rope came out often. We tied bowline knots off to rock notches and tree trunks. Handholds were small and slick, the boulders hanging over our heads, barely caught above us.

Laura extended past her capabilities and I saw her below me, grinding her teeth, cursing at the rocks that she clutched, fighting against her own weight. The place that had given her falling leaves was now ripping at her. She didn't want to fall, nervous and afraid, but her pack kept tugging, pulling her off balance.

At the top of a boulder field she came over a boulder's peak after Colin had left, hauling the weight of her pack up and slumping it against the ground. Sweat clung to her face like glass beads even in the coolness. Her lower lip trembled.

"I'm going to cry," she said, not even trying to catch her breath. "This is too much." Her head tilted back, pulling air into her mouth.

I looked at her, not saying anything, careful with my expression, not showing her any fear or expectation. We had a long way to go today before reaching a good stopping place. Her agreement with the land was being torn down.

"I can't keep doing this," she said.

I gave her a firm, lifesaver voice. "Look at me, Laura. You can't doubt yourself." But I saw her eyes and knew that anything I told her would be a distant mumble.

"I know, but this is too much for me. How far do we have until we're in a safe spot, someplace where I don't have to climb with this goddamned pack? Another thousand feet?"

"Maybe."

"Shit. Straight up? A thousand feet? I'm nerve-wracked. My legs and my arms are shaking. See?" She held her hand out, palm down, not for my benefit, but in front of her own eyes. "I can't even keep my hands still. Christ, how am I supposed to climb? I can't get out of this canyon."

I could not say anything to her. I did not move, my own pack heavy, my muscles shivering a bit.

She reached up to the pendant on her necklace, a Saint Christopher her mother had given her, the patron saint of lost children. She clutched it in her hand. She closed her eyes. When she opened them, her face was full of emotion. She nodded for me to go. I did. I heard her cave into tears behind me, frustrated and scared. I hunched back up behind a boulder out of sight and waited. When I heard her footsteps a few minutes later, I kept on.

I remembered visiting her once in her shoebox apartment in Portland. It was when she was working at the women's shelter and with sexually abused teens, plunging herself into the heart of human need and fear. In the hours after midnight in her apartment she lay curled on the floor sobbing, my arms around her as if I was hanging on to a bleeding, shot animal. Her jobs were becoming too much to bear. There was pain everywhere. People were killing each other in the city, ripping each other apart like trapped animals. She was left to die in her tiny room, death by the stabbing ache of humanity, while she forced herself to care for those coming in beaten by their husbands, for angry young boys who either had wild panic on their faces or the unquestioning expression of a predator. She cried in waves, her body heaving. I held her on the floor until she fell asleep, turning the anguish inward.

I checked back on Laura now and then, meeting her eyes as we climbed through the tiers of this canyon. She was not seeing me. She had made some sort of accord with the land after crying at the last boulder field. Her manner exuded sheer will, hand reaching ahead for a tree root, boot slammed into a hold to push herself up. I knew what was in her head right now. If this was the sanctuary she had come for, she would have to turn herself into a creature of the wilderness. She would have to pay, abandoning her fears and thoughts. She dug at the ground with every movement, tearing away the ponderous outside of herself.

The canyon tightened even more. It lurched into rock columns, quills standing five hundred feet over our heads. The very bottom of the canyon came down to a sliver. We waded through pools of cold water in dim light, our voices steely and full of echoes as we sent reports back and forth to each other. Finally we could not follow the bottom any longer and we climbed hand over hand up the side ledges, rising through fragile rungs of rock.

Colin was out of sight, far overhead, Laura twenty feet below me.

There came a crisp breaking sound. Rock from up high. I froze, looking up.

First I saw small ricochet pieces of rock firing out of the brush. Behind them was a single boulder the size of a car tire. It emerged as if bursting onto stage through a curtain. Colin had knocked it loose. It threw chunks of tree and other rock into the air. It was straight above us. I looked down to Laura.

I yelled, "*Rock!*"

She met my eyes. Full of sudden questions. She looked like a cat unexpectedly cornered.

No quick moves could be made with our feet tapped into these tiny, brittle holds. Not with sixty pounds on our backs. I looked up. The boulder catapulted into the air over my head.

I solidified both my feet and my hands, cinching them into cracks and tiny but solid holds. This way I had four points of contact. I could swivel away onto one or two of them for an instant rather than have my body taken out by the boulder. I added the weight of my pack to my instant thinking, how it would thrust me farther out. Any dodge would have to be a complete motion, parting and returning just in time with the boulder, no jarring.

But what about Laura? She didn't know this technique, the points of contact, the delicate parry of a body with a pack. She would hold fast, stubborn and angry, throwing dirty laundry at the rock with her eyes to knock it off course. I could not help her. It would pass in less than half a second.

The boulder hurtled two feet from my right shoulder, showering me with smaller pieces. Black-eye rocks. Slides of dust and dry oak leaves followed, washing my face. I did not have to shift any weight. It was a clean miss. I followed it over my shoulder, watching its fall toward Laura.

If it were to hit her, it would shear a limb, or explode through her rib cage. It would kill her. She did not move at all. Her eyes drilled the boulder as if challenging it. Her muscles solidified. From my vantage, it was about to strike her in the abdomen. I sucked air through my teeth, trying to stop time, pulling back on the boulder.

It passed her left knee by a few inches, going down with furious cracks and heaves as it collided with other objects.

Fear was in my mouth. It was a bite of a rotten, acidic orange. I breathed and buried my head in the cup between my chest and my shoulder.

The boulder was gone behind her as suddenly as it had arrived. Laura's body shivered. She did not turn to watch it break into smaller pieces below. Bold strokes of emotion displayed across her face, eyes wide. She bore the look of a person coming up from a plunge in ice water, almost drowned. This poisonous land had locked itself into her, and she was at that moment the clownfish, safe in these stinging arms, terrified and alive.

This country is filled with motion even when I think it is still. The boulders are all wishing to fall and the canyon holds them like a finger on the spring of a metal trap. Had I said that I never believed that the landscape has living intentions? That was perhaps something written without enough experience. The leaves here want to fall and spin as much as Laura wants to applaud for them. The irregularity and extremity of this landscape makes these paths of movement even more apparent than would a gentler place. Every object pushes against the other, wind against rock against leaf against cliff. We could feel the vibrations as we traveled. They changed our emotions and the way we moved. They left Laura with the quick demeanor of an animal as she climbed below me, keeping on after the boulder had passed.

With my waist anchored by a rope back to a tree root, I hauled up Laura's pack on another rope after hauling mine. Laura teetered below, her boot tips on a hold, her arm stretched up to push her pack toward me. I saw her face, the strain as she shoved with the longest reach of her fingers, her expression questionless. For that moment I did not see us as tiny, alien figures within a colossal and fierce landscape. Instead, we were boulders and leaves. We followed paths of desire like everything else here.

Eventually we reached a broad inner shelf that strung along both sides of the canyon. On it we found a township of cliff dwellings, remnants of the last act of human desire in this canyon. These were mostly two- and three-story buildings with broad timbers for support, great adobe walls that rose around us as we entered. Many were in prime condition with artwork painted in reds and whites in interior rooms, a few with ceilings caved into floors of rubble. Some of the wall plaster had been artfully crafted: they had used woven mats instead of their hands, so that the plaster had the visual exactness of textile. There was cotton on the floors, dirty wads of it knotted into sticks and wood-rat droppings.

After several hours of delving into the site, I came into one room and found Laura. She sat in front of a doorway that had been completely sealed with mortar. Her face was steady and thoughtful. "What is this?" she asked.

"The door? Probably some change in function for a room."

"They sealed the room off," she said, her voice flat.

"Maybe it became storage."

"No. They sealed it off. Something happened."

I watched her face for clues. She was far inside of herself. "What do you mean?"

"There was something in this room, some violence or madness that they had to close off so that no one would have to bear it again."

I sat down in the rubble near her, studying the door. "I don't know what it means," I said.

"There was violence, wasn't there?"

How had she made this connection? I had never thought of violence and sealed doors as having anything to do with each other. I had until now been looking at this cliff dwelling as a lone-standing town. Her question reminded me that there were outside forces, elements that drove people here. Her mention of violence and the closed entry made me oddly uncomfortable. What was she seeing here?

"Violence?" I asked.

"There was violence, right?"

"Yes," I said, caught off guard. "There was a lot of violence.

Especially near the end. Horrible things were happening north of here, a ritualized sort of warfare and entire pueblos set fire with their rooms stuffed full of people, burned alive."

"Mmm," she muttered, a pensive recognition. "But this was far enough away? Far from the cities of the times?"

"I don't know if it was or not. Maybe there is a time when nothing is far enough away."

I told her what I knew about the documentation. The burned skeleton of a young woman from this era, likely a teenager, had been found in an excavated pueblo southwest of here. Her right arm had been completely broken off midway below her shoulder while she was still alive. Excavators could not find the rest of her arm, as if it had been tossed up for grabs. In the top of her head was an oval hole the size and shape of a typical stone axe tip. The skeleton of a man was found nearby with an arrowhead lodged midway between his knee and ankle. Around this man and young woman were the extremely scattered remains of about one hundred others. This was only an example. There were numerous such sites.

Evidence like this had been surfacing lately. Archaeologists were abandoning outdated, simpler notions of Native Americans who did not engage in organized warfare or long-distance politics in the last thousand years. They were bringing evidence to the surface, volumes of data on victims of organized violence.

Laura seemed stirred by this evidence. The frustration of it. She saw the repetitive nature, her own experiences in the city. "It is difficult to imagine that sort of thing here," she said. "I don't mean to sound idealistic. I think this place has its own sort of violence, but it's not barbaric. It's boulders and cliffs. It doesn't have to seal up its doors to forget things."

I looked at the closed door. There were handprints in the mortar. I could see where the makers had put their weight against fresh mud, forcing it tight into a space that had once been an opening. For Laura, the monster was on the other side, something left there by people seven hundred years ago.

Laura followed my eyes to the door. "These canyons won't cover up our madness, though. We bring everything with us when we come."

I watched Laura. I watched her eyes, how they never went dull. She was becoming something, an electrified being, tightly wound. The terrain pounded at her, wearing her down to her core. She told stories in camp, horrible stories like the one of a woman shoved through a sliding glass door by the man who loved her dearly. She culled through each of her images, boiling down her life until I could see the fear in her, fear that there was something fragile at the center that she did not want harmed. Like all of us.

We carried ourselves, our stories and fears and heavy equipment, through canyon after canyon, a banging caravan of travelers. On the twentieth day we divided to find our own ways through a canyon. Moving was slow work, stepping from one loose object to another, quickly calculating balance before stepping again, never staying on a foot long enough to be thrown by a loose boulder or a bad hold.

I was up on an east-facing slope, almost sheer enough to be a cliff, snagged with loose rocks and small ledges. I thought I was alone when I heard Colin's voice. He said my name. I looked around but did not see him. He had sounded as if he was nearby.

"Wave your arms," I said.

He did and I saw him on the opposite side of the canyon, ten thousand boulders away. With a soft, serious tone he said, "You need to come here." His voice sounded surprisingly close, echoing sharply.

I gave everything a quick glance. "You're way over there," I objected.

"You need to come here now."

I weighed the tone of his voice. He had found something.

Seeking a fast way to reach him, I put my trust on a big handhold. Like dry pastry it broke in my hand and I tumbled backward. My boots flopped down the wall, knocking rocks loose. I hit a slight shelf, landing on my side. I grabbed whatever I could with my elbows, my shoulders, my fingers. This stayed me. Dust and rocks came down. I covered my head with my hands. Rocks broke over my knuckles, continuing below me into the canyon floor, turning the place loud with echoes.

When the rocks stopped, I looked at my hands. Cuts on my knuckles were white with sand, the blood immediately thick and dry as it came out covered with powder. There would be dark places on my body, maps of bruises. I did not wait to test my heart, to let the adrenaline sieve out through my blood and organs. I kept with the momentum, crossing the canyon to reach Colin and his find.

When I arrived, midway up the other side, he seemed worried and excited at once. I leaned my back on a boulder to support my weight, tilting my head up to swallow air.

"I saw you fall," he said.

I nodded.

"You okay?"

I nodded again.

"Catch your breath," he said, his voice firm.

When the heat receded from my cheeks, Colin said, "I found something in a cave."

"What is it?"

"Have you caught your breath?"

"Yes."

"Follow me."

On the way to his cave we came across three large pieces of pottery broken in the rocks. They bore detailed black-line paintings on a clean, white background. The scrupulousness was startling, the black terse in its outlines: tiny triangles, a squared spiral, curves and lines, the style known as Salado Polychrome. Colin urged me to put the pottery down. I did.

He took me up a wall to an overhang that descended into a cave. It was narrow and tall, a natural keyhole doorway. At the mouth were three drapes of honeycombs, cakes of wax extending nearly four feet toward the floor. They had been abandoned and only the casings of dead bees were left on the ground. He gestured for me to enter. I slipped around him, beside the hives. In the attic light of the cave I could see on the floor pieces of broken honeycomb and dark-and-light patches. I let my eyes adjust.

The images came slowly. Light and dark became black-on-white painted pottery, broken rounds of bowls. A small, flat stone became an axe head. Two fat knobs of fallen honeycomb changed into a pair of baskets partially buried in the debris. It was an ancient storage room, a supply cache. I waited until I could see clearly before walking farther.

I came to one of the baskets. When I turned to look at Colin, his face was solemn but still holding back intoxication, as if he could not fit the two sensations together at the same time. He looked at me, to the baskets, back at me.

"They haven't been moved," he said. "This is how I found them."

I had never before seen a pre-Columbian basket without its tag and catalog number written in black ink. Here in this crowded little cave, I had an overwhelming sense of context, something I'd never experienced in a museum. The baskets had not been removed from the flow of this wilderness. I settled into the floor on my knees. The baskets were unmarked, belonging to no one. They sat unmoved like a pair of shoes in a lost and found box, the owners never to return. They had been left exactly like this. By what hands? What was this cave?

Colin had found a time machine clogged with random pieces of eras, baskets and pottery caught in the wheels of the machine, causing it to stop here in front of my eyes. Humans had tangled themselves into the processes of this landscape. They had found a secure location and filled it with their belongings, as if trying to hold themselves in place.

Cracks in the cave wall were streaked with the gloss of wood-rat urine. It smelled like a rodent cellar in here. Nobody had been here for centuries, at least not as far as I could tell.

This nearest basket was oriented toward the entrance. Frail light caught its narrowing, circular mouth leaving it black inside. It was far enough into the cave that crouched over it I did not even cast a shadow. Minute by minute my eyes adjusted, giving me more details of the weaving. It had been a water basket, its weave cinched down, the exterior painted with pitch from a pine tree. The body was plump and round. Two wooden handles had been webbed into its side with a leather strap. I moved to the second basket, finding it to be nearly identical in shape and weave to the first. It was also meant for carrying water, supported by a head strap run through the wooden handles.

The cave was a library of human presence. We would disturb nothing in it. I felt the dirt. It was parched. Colin would agree without second thought, as would Laura: no one else would know of this place. We would never come back here again.

The baskets, made from woven strips of squawbush, were of Apache origin. The Apache culture and the older cliff dwellers were unrelated to each other. There were no family ties or trade routes between them. The Apache, like the Navajo, are Athabascan. Nomadic people, at least before confinement to reservations, they migrated down from the Arctic, coming to a land that was harsh and arid, but ripe for them after being mostly vacated by a prior civilization. When they arrived they were as culturally discontinuous to this region as I now am.

Meanwhile, the people who left this scattered pottery were ancient, their southwestern bloodlines taking them back into the tens of thousands of years. The crossing of three cultures felt strong in this chamber. Apache, cliff dwellers, and ourselves. I thought, How long will this go on? How many more will there be? Civilizations come and go, sending their exiles, their refugees, and their lunatics out to this land of canyons, the one place that will guarantee their remains. Laura, Colin, and I had come right on schedule.

In the last days of our month we split up, taking with us only the most necessary equipment. We needed a couple days apart from one another before rejoining and completing our trek. The things we had carried for the past twenty-eight days felt burdensome, each item keeping us a step removed from this place. We wished to strip down, to go alone, shrugging our human cycles as best we could, coming closer to the other cycles that wheeled around us. I walked north carrying a small pack—a sleeping bag, jacket, a warm hat, and a bag of raisins and nuts, enough food to feed my muscles. I wanted to become a naked basket, to be handed over to the country.

I came into a slot canyon in the late afternoon, just as heavy clouds descended from the south. The wind turned cold. It was the second week of December, remarkably colder than when we began in November. I walked with my hands sliding against either wall, sixty feet below the top of this canyon, a couple thousand feet below the highest rim. Clouds snagged and tore on the earth far over my head, pulling in a storm.

The walls bent across each other, worked here at the bottom with patterns of old water flows. Then came a pool of stagnant, black water. I could not climb around it, so I removed my clothes. I shuffled into the middle of the pool, my belongings held over my head. The water was blisteringly cold as it reached my chest. It came to my armpits, to my neck. I felt my way through with my toes, keeping my head aloft.

The pool went on, out of sight around bends. Sometimes it was short and deep, forcing me to swim, other times fifty yards long and only knee-deep, my bare feet tentatively studying the mud and stone-beaded ground. I was shivering violently when I came out of the far end.

The storm gained force. It began spitting rain into the canyon. The rain quickly turned to a light sleet, popping soft spots of ice onto my shoulders and my back. At a wide area I got my clothes on over wet skin and scrambled up the side of the canyon to a tall, shallow cave.

The cave had no level floor, only a staircase of ledges. It was just enough to get me out of the weather. I built a small fire from twigs, taking them from what looked like the collapsed nest of an owl. At first, the fire was only smoke. I leaned down, blowing lightly at an ember in the center. Then flames lifted, wrapping up through the kindling. Hunching over, feeding it twigs, the heat rose across my face. As night came, sleet turned to snow, whisping into the cave with the wind, landing cold on my cheeks.

I thought of Laura and her search for immunity in this wilderness. She was finding it right now, and it was real, so real that it was soaking into her skin. I imagined her awake all night, damp and freezing somewhere beneath the bough of a juniper tree, despising and loving this wind at the same instant.

For me, this was sufficient shelter. The storm, and protection from it, offered serenity. It was the feeling of having a home, a safe place within a grand array of cycles and landforms. My small catch of flames lit the full height of the cave. Sleep would not be comfortable tonight. I would have to fit into one of these shelves, tucking my free arm to keep my weight from turning me over the edge. Even so, it was worth this sense of shelter and composure. In two days we would be out of here. We would hitch a ride along the nearest dirt road, returning to our parked car in the back of a ranch truck, crouched like inmates, hands folded against driving snow. For now, that was far away.

After an hour or so I let the fire burn to a soft illumination of coals. My hands kept sinking closer to them in the cold. The embers sputtered and brightened as breezes came through with feathers of snow. When the light was finally gone, I was left in a dark hole in the bottom of the canyon, the storm moaning across it like wind across a glass bottle.

I thought of the balcony ruin that Laura and I had reached the year before, looking across this region on a clear day. At that moment I was in the center of the land looking outward, as curious as a tourist. Now I was in the center looking inward. I saw darkness. I heard the storm, the intricacy of its wind defining for me the shape of the canyon. I was down in a crack in the land, and I felt as if I could stick my hand deeper from here, opening a hole into the earth and myself, finding my way beneath this outer flesh of sanctuary. I imagined a place that is not built for protection, a perplexing landscape beyond this one where I might be able to find its covenants. The land I had envisioned as a child was a simple one, a fortress terrain that satisfied my desire for curiosity and safety. But I have grown older, learning that this land goes deeper than I can imagine.

I picked up my last dry stick, urging the coals a little brighter, wondering about the place I would need to go next, and about leaving the harbor of these huge canyons, my childhood dreams. The coals rolled over, glowing orange beneath. I pulled the stick out before it began to smoke.

I had an image in my head. A monk sitting beside a roaring river. After waiting in that terrible, alluring sound, for years maybe, he stands and walks to the edge. He drops his cloak and stands naked. Then he walks in and is swept away.

My river was this land. I had long wished that I could enter the cogs and gears of this earth, abandoning myself to the very devices that power this wild spell. The route to get there was not here. It was through the desert beyond here, where these exterior forests are shed. I needed a place excoriated by wind and floods, driven down to only the most principal shapes, the monk's river.

But I was perfectly comfortable with my coals for the moment. I did not want to move or do something as ridiculous as abandon my cave during a night's storm. The land outside the cave was huge in the dark, infinite. The storm began wailing, plugging the ledges below me with snow, sealing me in.

PASSAGE

Grand Canyon, Arizona

There is a place that would have been as smooth as Kansas had it been left alone. It would have been a gentle dome of land covered in forests, meadows, and open pastures. Instead, the ground has fallen out from under it, sending it into the desert below. Flash floods have ravaged it, and the Colorado River cuts into its heart, sculpting a mile-deep ingress that lies nearly three hundred miles long. Within this, crannies are carved. Passages lead down as if burning through the crust, diminutive wedges that unfold the land.

Erosion is fast in this place. Each day portions of cliff avalanche into thunder and dust. The hundreds, thousands of canyons within are even now carving themselves away, writhing among each other like snakes in a bag. It is called the Grand Canyon. It is just north and west of the Mogollon Rim, in dry country.

The highland chasms of northern Mexico and the canyon sprawls in the rim country of central Arizona are lumbering giants among land-forms, crude in their boldness. The Grand Canyon, on the other hand, is like splitting open a scabrous rock and finding inside a crystal, a place constructed of orderly angles and facets.

I came to this place because of its routes. They are threads streaking through cliffs and inner grottoes, days of narrow shelves and bridges built of fallen boulders. Traveling along these routes is like studying the skeleton of an animal, the way joints hinge off of each other. But they are not easy to find. The place is a lesson in riddles, a two-thousand-square-mile conundrum of stone where only certain ledges or crevices connect one place to the next, and the rest, most of it, is a dead end, a land of cliffs.

In my first far-ranging travels in the Grand Canyon, months spent in untrailed portions of its interior, I was in a constant state of invention. Painstakingly searching for passages, I sometimes took weeks to make relatively short distances, my days sprinkled with backtracks and failed detours. Other places, the Mogollon Rim canyons for example, allowed free wandering from place to place, and easy observations of my surroundings. Here, I had to know every type of rock, how it would change the course of my day, where it would leave me by nightfall.

Grand Canyon travel is much like a concentrated game of pool where you are concerned not only with the angle of the shot and where the targeted ball will go, but where all of the other balls will come to rest and how they will influence the next turn. Each canyon lies in a field of intricate relationships and I walked through them constantly aware, using geological maps instead of topographic ones, rappelling into tomblike caverns with the proper gear on hand so that I could suddenly turn and inch my way back up the rope. I was down in the machinery of the planet.

As I traveled I thought of Aboriginal songlines across the western deserts of Australia, and Native lyrics and drumming used to steer through fjordic waters of British Columbia. Generations of knowledge had been employed to find the way through. Setting out across the greater landscape beyond familiar home territory, people took with them stories passed down that told how to navigate. I felt left out of this ritual, pushing my way alone through a staggering assemblage of canyons.

I once met a man doing research on the island of Maui, trying to retrace an ancient pilgrimage across the barrens of the Haleakala volcano, and his talk of tribal ways reminded me of what I wished for in the Grand Canyon. There were courses of travel, he said, that could only be defined by how they were embedded into cultural life. He had spent a year engaging with native elders, gaining their trust so that he could hear of their routes. The elders, he discovered, had nothing tangibly recorded about how to cross this place of windswept and waterless cinders. It was all told in song, every turn and path of the pilgrimage. Their maps were made of stories, their routes defined by music.

I wanted this sort of cultural relevance within my own travels, to not live and move entirely in isolation. I left the Grand Canyon and went looking for its elders. I took a tape recorder and notebook with me and sat with older travelers, asking them about the essence of this extremely rugged landscape, learning from them how they found their ways through without the aid of engineered trails. We opened maps together and shared stories, and I took assiduous notes, putting an oral geography down on paper.

When I found that two of the most accomplished route finders were mathematicians, I was enchanted by the notion that there might be a penetrable, arithmetic array to this place, something that could be named, that we could explain to each other. I have long considered math to be another form of storytelling. It is a way of communicating that takes an impracticable landscape and expresses its order. It is a way of navigating the far places, and it could very well be a code of route-finding.

Harvey Butchart is one of these mathematicians. His doctoral thesis dealt with extending spiral helices in Euclidean space into any number of dimensions (when he told me this I dutifully wrote it into my notebook and have not since had the faintest idea what it means). I met him when he was ninety-one years old. He had walked twelve-thousand miles through the Grand Canyon uncovering routes, many of which had not been used since the Anasazi culture seven hundred years earlier. I knew that if I could talk with him, if I could listen to his voice, he would make a line of contact for me, a way of seeing the Grand Canyon. Among circles of northern Arizona travelers he is known as the cardinal route finder. Walking twelve-thousand miles within a place consisting mostly of cliffs and only fifty miles of maintained trails is a remarkable feat.

I wanted to know of his routes not so much so that I could follow them, but so that I could know what he had done. I wanted to hear about traveling into the outer lands, legends of the sort that every culture carries, journeys into the boundless country.

I finally asked Harvey about math. I had worked up a theory in my head, that navigating a complicated strand of logic was very similar to working through unknown routes in the Grand Canyon. There were proofs and theorems with every step, givens in certain rock formations, logarithms carved out of canyon floors, sums and solutions in arriving at the other end. I gave him an abbreviated version of this and asked if he believed it to be true. He waved away my question as if it had a foul smell. He said that math is math, route finding is route finding.

"You say you play chess twice a day," I said to him.

He gave me a professor's look, one reserved for a romantically misled student. He said with his elderly, trembling voice, "Not the same thing."

Instead of flooding me with his brilliance in mathematics, he settled into a story and I abandoned that line of inquiry. He told me that he had gone into the Grand Canyon with a former student, twenty-three years old. He was forty-four then. You know how difficult it can get in there, he said, long walks, narrow ledges, the river at the bottom cold and full of rapids. The student, the friend, was not as adept as he. His story progressed as many Grand Canyon stories do, the travel becoming more challenging, dangers cropping up, fear of death, mistakes made. His friend was desperate at one point while they entered the river with their packs to get downstream. Harvey tried to help, but could not. He had to save himself.

He said, "I started a little fire, made some soup and tried to eat enough to keep up my strength, but that was pretty hard to do the way I felt."

"The way you felt?" I asked.

"His body was never found."

"What?"

"I went through a state of depression for nearly six months," he said, clicking his dentures into place, as was his habit when telling stories. He looked at me and saw that I was deeply concerned, that I had not expected such a loss. Reassuring me, he said, "But I did keep going out there."

The conversation moved on to other routes and stories without pause, but this one dominated my mind. His friend had died forty-seven years earlier and Harvey had continued his work, discovering more routes as if uncovering artifacts. In the years since he told me this story I have opened every one of its words and found inside a way of moving. Like a map slyly recorded within a song, a solution within a math problem, his story gave me everything a person would need to know in order to make it through the Grand Canyon. Whatever path Harvey had found in this complex and difficult place, it is stronger than death.

The other Grand Canyon elder that I sought was George Steck. He received his Ph.D. in theoretical math from the University of California at Berkeley. I first traveled with him when he was seventy-three years old. We carried a couple nights of gear through fields of boulders and a few hand-over-hand ledges from the rim of the Grand Canyon to the river. There we stripped naked and swam in the Colorado River.

George described his routes to me with a steady, comprehensive tone, telling me about places of incredible hazard and reward. He had walked the entire length of the Grand Canyon when he was fifty-seven years old, in eighty days, all of it done in the puzzling confines of the inner reaches. I had seen some of his routes before, and had used a number of them, his meager catwalks and handholds. They were like spider's silk, lines across the landscape that were not visible until I touched them.

The second time George and I traveled together, he was seventy-five. He knew of a route few people had ever seen, one found by pale-ontologists studying caves in the northern reaches of the Grand Canyon. The research team had come across the yawn of a brief and extremely steep canyon carved into limestone. Up one of its walls they found something unexpected, the rickety wooden remains of an Anasazi stairway, a permanent ladder system seven or eight hundred years old. They climbed from there, finding a succession of caves that laced through the cliff to the next highest rim. George thought that I should know where this place is, telling me that any route that slips so perfectly through an insurmountable cliff is one worth following. It was a streak of grace through the turmoil, a story told within the land-scape like the drum through the straits and sounds of British Columbia's coast. He said it would likely be the last time he would be able to show anyone.

We were at the rim of the Grand Canyon in early November, preparing to start down this route. Six of us huddled around an evening fire, the wind unusually cold. Bright little embers scrambled out with the gusts, driven across hardpan limestone to the edge. They shot over, bright comets with thousands of feet to go before touching ground.

Tequila and cigarettes. Stories about routes and long journeys into the Grand Canyon. George had come with two friends, John and Tom, from Albuquerque. I came with Regan Choi. She did not crouch beside the fire with the rest of us. She stood just out of earshot, watching the landscape below draw from view into the night.

Also here was Colin Wann. He was the tallest, even taller than George, who was well above six feet. George stood over the fire with his arms tight against his body to conserve heat. Dominating his eyes were feathered wings for eyebrows. Professor eyebrows. "Cold," he said, laying the word out like a sturdy punctuation mark. Snow was coming off the high country behind us, promising to get here by morning. He rarely uses more words than he needs. Without saying anything else, he walked off to sleep somewhere.

Conversations continued, wood jostled around to accept the flame. Tom talked about having just ended a nine-year relationship, and about this past week of agonizing phone calls with the woman in question. "Coming to do the wormhole with Steck," he laughed painfully, sipping his tequila. "That'll sober anyone up."

The wormhole. That is what George called this route. He said that it was quintessential, the entire region leading down to a critical move no wider than my own hips, and if I did not yet understand how to move with ease in this inscrutable landscape, I would now learn. I had seen this very section of canyon before and had abandoned it as completely inaccessible. Where I had assumed unapproachable earth, I would now know a way, learning how to slip from emptiness into a place, turning it into memory and possibility, turning it into myself.

Snow arrived in the morning. Nothing heavy. It blew like soft confetti, heading every direction. At the lip of the Grand Canyon, it shot straight up, driven by a rising wind. We all stumbled around getting gear ready, bodies hunched from the cold—Regan over there braiding her hair for efficiency, Colin crouched waiting, his pack ready to go long before anyone else's, Tom and John hovering over clutched coffee. George was off pissing into a heap of blackbrush. He looked like a tall and slender statue, even with the curvature that old men take when urinating in the cold. He had the perfect build for a dedicated Grand Canyon traveler. I felt like a tree stump next to him.

Everyone performed morning duties, including me, standing with cold hands jammed in my pockets, looking over the gulf before me. Hardly anything grew down there. There were no forests, and no thick groves of trees. It was mostly bare rock, the product of a high desert too hot in the summer and too cold in the winter. And it was immense. The Grand Canyon has always scared me a bit with its size. Still, I could see from the rim delicate lines of canyons presenting their unquestionable patterns: rims and paths and uninterrupted cliffs. The internal form of the earth distilled in front of me and I sensed that I did not end at my skin, but headed beyond, down into these eroding yet inflexible shapes.

Standing here, I could not be defined solely by my body or my own thoughts. My senses went out like a net tossed across immeasurable distances. We would find our way here.

This northern limit of the Grand Canyon has as abrupt an edge as I've seen anywhere on the planet. Step back fifty feet and visual knowledge of any canyon at all is erased, swallowed in a broad plain bordered by flanks of red sandstone cliffs. Even when I could not see this interior canyon, knowledge of it had weight, as if it were a physical presence pushing against me. Or, more aptly, pulling on me.

Before starting, George led us over to the head of another canyon a short distance south, showing us a route he had used a couple decades ago. He wanted us to know about it, in case we ever needed a way down here. It was a big chunk of Kaibab limestone broken away from its parent foundation, leaving a discreet course to the next level down. And from there, George said, there was a way.

I followed as much of the way as I could with my eyes. Standing still, hands remaining in my pockets, I traced off the Kaibab limestone, down through steps of the Toroweap formation, stalling at the drops of Coconino sandstone until finding a way down to the rubble slopes of Hermit shale, then into the staggered cliffs and benches of the Supai formation. They sound like just a run of names, senseless geology, but each strata is distinct. Hermit shale, red as a rusted Edsel, snaps to pieces under foot. Coconino is white and smooth and there is no way down its exposed face without ropes or adequate crevices. The Tapeats, colored in cranberry and chocolate, is a hive of overhangs and ledges, an easy place to get stranded.

Harvey Butchart's specialty was the Redwall strata, the largest obstacle, a band of seven-hundred-foot cliffs that stand like a Great Wall throughout most of the Grand Canyon. That is where my eyes stopped this morning, at the upper margin of the Redwall. I couldn't find a route from there. I turned to George. "Is there a way down the Redwall?"

He gave me a sly, knowing look. "Yes. With a three-hundred-foot rappel." His voice was gravelly, upturning the last word into a question. A smart voice. An asking voice. "If you call that a way down."

"I don't," I said.

While we all stood gawking, Colin's eyes were on the ground. He came up with the circular base of a ceramic pot, gray and corrugated. Cooking pot. The shard was the size of a playing card, curved in the middle and rounded at the edges. We passed it around. Its underside was freckled with ice. They knew about this route too, people from long ago. The Anasazi.

George took us north again, and we loaded packs heading off for the passage to the wormhole, the Anasazi route that should get us to the Colorado River after a couple days of walking. We reached a place, not actually the head of a canyon, just a place. The smoothness of the land fell into the maw of the first high cliffs. We entered here, where acres of stone platforms had broken away, leaning over the open space below. Massive boulders had rolled free, some landing five hundred feet lower, others caught near the top, locked against each other. The whole thing is out of proportion for a human scale. We were ridiculously small.

There were boulders surrounded by boulders, huge pieces of stone as large as city blocks. Between these were smaller ones resting at the last angle of repose, steady, but anxious to fall, like a breath about to be taken. Some did roll as we walked. Loosened by our weight, they tumbled into plumes of bright dust, picking up more rocks, sending them down. The shout. "Rock!" Everybody directly below leaping out of its path. Others out of range staring, enthralled. The first two hours were punctuated by these warning shouts of rock and the powder-flash smell of impact and sparks.

George moved slowly. Not painfully, just slowly. He took rests, palms spread on his thighs, his antiquated frame pack shoving at his old back. He used aluminum poles to help his balance. They clicked as they touched the next solid rock down.

I had trailed him with my notebook in hand before, sketching his words, his replies to my questions.

"Why do you do this, wandering around such a challenging place?"
"I like it."
"But why here? Why such a unique task?"
"It's not unique, I just put one foot in front of the other."
"That's not what I'm asking, George. Why is a theoretical mathematician also a pioneer route finder? Why do you walk for eighty days and find satisfaction with some boulder-filled chute that gets you from one place to the next? It must not have been a common hobby among people at the lab."

He always answered with humility, even though he sensed the answer I was trying to find and the next questions I would ask. He became a friend instead of a subject, patiently hearing my inquiries.

"Why, George?"

"Because I want to, Craig, the same for you, right? We're driven by what we want."

At the Sandia Laboratory in New Mexico, he had worked with the mathematical principles of low-flying aircraft, delving into his postulations the same way astronomers explore black holes, the way physicists play with leptons and quarks. His conclusions were reached with logic, pages and books and tomes of logic.

"Ultimately," he once told me, "I found a very simple, beautiful formula for some very complicated expressions."

He could have just as easily been talking about his time in the Grand Canyon. I moved ahead of George, dropping through boulders, taking handholds, lower and lower, the rim rising away from me, the next rim down coming closer. We were descending into the void.

When I reached the brink of the Coconino sandstone, I caught up with the others and waited, pack released to the ground. George came eventually, sitting away on his own. We called him over to sit at the edge and toss rocks down with us. His assuaging laugh answered us.

He wasn't going to travel any farther than this. That is what his laugh said. Even though he had packed supplies for a number of days and carried them this far, he was not going to make it. Too old. Too tired. Too far. Too steep. He just sat there, leaning against his pack, looking over the canyons below. He said nothing.

About ten minutes after John and Tom jetted off our precipice into the boulder fields below, the remainder of us began collecting our packs. Except for George.

"I'm not going to make this one," he announced with a casual tone. "It's harder than I remembered it."

We were awkwardly quiet for a moment. George was not awkward. He had decided. "I'll give you my map and tell you what I know. That should at least get you to the right place."

Still, we were quiet. Regan was the first. "How do you feel going back alone?"

"It's easier than coming down. I'll go slow. I'd rather that everybody gets to the wormhole. That is what we are here for. Right?"

I felt a knife cutting the tether between George and a bunch of children. We were being dropped into the din, while the one who knew how to negotiate would rise away. "What about making it down to the Esplanade?" I asked, looking over my shoulder about six hundred feet down. "We'll plan to set a camp there."

"No," he said. "I need to turn back here. You should be able to find the wormhole." He brought a topographic map out of a plastic bag and unfolded it in front of us. The map was a tangle of lines, entire elevations erased by cliffs. He talked. I nodded, and asked a few questions. He talked about talus slopes and places to contour over. His index finger ran across the map. "You get down in this drainage and there are two towers of Redwall standing in front of you. Between the towers, beneath them. It's on the south side, but you can only see it from the north. There are quite a few caves visible in there, so you have to get the right one. And you won't need all the rope you brought, although I'd sure want it there."

Even with his finger on the map, exactly on the wormhole, I knew that it would not be so easy. There are so many landmarks that it is nearly impossible to triangulate with a compass. This place is a hall of mirrors.

He didn't once look into my eyes to verify that I had any idea what he was talking about. He just delivered the message, folded the map, stuck it back in its plastic bag, and handed the bag to me.

"Good luck," he said.

We slept that night far within the Grand Canyon, meager dabs of snow landing in the creases of my eyelids. They didn't keep me awake, but I was aware each time a new one fell. Suddenly there was a deep, loud sound. I opened my eyes. Thunder, I thought. But it was too percussive for thunder. Not the right time of year. I could feel it through my back. Regan sleepily said, "Rockfall," the way somebody says, "Dogs in the garbage can." I relaxed. Some large chunk of territory had slipped, maybe thousands of tons. Somewhere out there. The land was moving, breathing. It was quiet again.

Cold morning, then. Long bolts of light spread through the notches of other canyons. Walking around to warm my muscles I found three broken arrowheads in different places on the ground. We had chosen a good place to sleep, an Anasazi stopover on the way down. I walked to the edge over the next drop and sat, pulling out my notebook and pen, fumbling with chilled fingers. Writing, getting it down that there had been a rockfall during the night, I heard an explosion and my head snapped up. Everyone jumped, in the middle of coffee, or scraping oatmeal out of a metal cup. They came to the edge and watched.

On the other side of the canyon, adjacent to where we now stood, a piece of the high rim, Kaibab limestone, was breaking away. Concussions shot through every nearby canyon. Somebody said, "Holy shit." I agreed, but couldn't say it just then. Colin leapt from behind a boulder and stood on top of it, watching.

The canyon wall had cracked open, losing its facing. Pieces of wall multiplied in the collapse, sending up clouds and shoots of dust, smaller car-sized boulders cartwheeling into the air on odd trajectories. It was not the dirty, fouled dust of smaller rockslides. This was white smoke, pure pulverized limestone. The dust sank a couple thousand feet, following the avalanche of boulders. Some of it billowed high, crossing into the new sunlight while the rest sank toward the bottom.

I was suddenly alert with a vision of consequence, scales tipping, weight delivered, the clockwork gears of the Grand Canyon spinning into motion. Maybe it had been a shift in morning temperature, ice melting from around a linchpin boulder; maybe a few sand grains plucked out by a breeze, triggering the slide. I had many times heard cliff falls out here, as close as next door and from so far away I wasn't sure I had heard anything at all. Such sudden events in an uninhabited outback bring up the old, assumptive riddle, if a tree falls in a forest and no one is around to hear it. . . . Of course it makes a sound. It is perhaps even louder, more percussive because of its isolation.

To witness such a private and cataclysmic event as this is to pass into a different sense of time and space. The idea that our presence might be of any consequence at this moment in this far land is quieted. We were watching the earth fall into place, new routes forming in front of us, crystalline lines of passage shaping out of an act of sheer chaos.

The eruption continued downward, spilling from rim to rim, picking up new sections of cliff, cascading down and detonating at the next platform below, breaking off huge corners and starting the plunge again. In the end, the last fresh boulders rolled into their resting places. The dust drifted for miles and faded. The sound faded with a couple of sharp cracks, then nothing.

"Ah," I said, finally, dismayed.

John turned around, heading back to his gear to pack for the day. "What was that all about?" he asked.

There doesn't need to be a reason. We were in a land of sudden metamorphosis. It is not something we worry about.

We loaded gear on our backs and climbed into the Supai formation, spreading out one by one until somebody shouted, finding a way down. We all funneled back to that spot and climbed. The Supai is like this. Rather than being a solid cliff, it is a stack of benches, each one too sheer and too tall to easily climb. Slabs of boulders everywhere, deep red and grainy. Every crack and handhold defined whether a route could be followed or not. A single ledge, the only path, might be barely deep enough to hold the edges of our boots.

We plunged through these interior levels of the Grand Canyon, gasping, our air bubbles racing thousands of feet back to the surface through dry, rarefied air. Farther and farther inside. We could finally see canyons opening in the Redwall limestone below. Each canyon was dark and gray, narrow as a knife cut. They were heavy with shadows and blind curves dropping to who knows where. If the rest of the Grand Canyon is made of rock, then the canyons of the Redwall are made of seduction.

By noon we walked out of the wind-fed vastness of the upper country into the cavernous Redwall limestone. Pipe-cleaner canyons carved into the rock. I withdrew the map, figuring out what George had said, leading us down farther. We found the two towers of limestone he had told us about. They stood like pointed bedposts—seventy, eighty feet tall. As we approached, a ravine appeared between us and them. We came closer and the ravine breached open. It was more of a pit with cliffs for walls, scraped and carved from our feet to the floor. Nobody said anything for some time. We just looked straight into it as if gathered at the edge of a crater. Rather than exiting toward the river in regular fashion, this pit of a canyon burrowed down and made an arch for its outflow, a gaping hole a hundred feet tall, the towers standing to either side.

My mind was consumed by the motion around me, by visions of erosion and sequences, one covering stripped after another. What is revealed is an interior landscape that will never be divulged by a map or a photograph. It defines a person's vision, how one will move or pause. I know that every place has this. I have witnessed it in the heavy forests of Washington's Olympic Peninsula and across the unbroken plains of central Alberta, something not so much seen as sensed. It is something transitory, a moment when the tone of light and the shape of the horizon, perhaps the sudden sound of an animal or wind, meet at one place, revealing the indwelling landscape.

Here, the land is beginning to be pulled inside out. This inward territory comes to the surface, disclosing what other, more gentle landscapes might save for only fleeting instances. I came to the surface with it. The net of senses I had thrown out drew tighter. Everything that I looked at or heard was full of meaning, routes and dead ends, wind defining an entering canyon just out of my view, small caves beaming with intrigue, a sense of quickness to erosion, places that would collapse with very little provocation.

Looking into this massive hole, Tom asked, "Did he talk about a rounded drainage like this?"

"I don't think so," I said. "But there are the towers."

Colin stuck his head farther over. "It's pretty sheer. I'm not liking going over this lip straight down. This is the place for sure?"

I stared for a moment, caught more in fascination with the place than in looking for an answer. "Yes, for sure."

Colin turned around, smashing his hand against his forehead. "Aw, man," he said.

"There's a way," I said, mustering a convincing tone. "There's a route down here. It's always like this. You know. The best routes, you can't even see them."

Always like this. If you know the routes, you can sail through this country. If you don't, you stammer and fall. I imagine that among the Anasazi, the finding of a new route, the establishing of a trail, was a major feat of convenience and survival. If an Anasazi community did not know the routes, there was no trade, no game, no water. The land you could see in the distance but couldn't reach was nowhere. Finding a new route was also a major feat of relationship with the land.

These routes are my lines of connection with the place beyond my body, the surrounding universe; they are necessary anchor points without which I would recoil into a shell, exiled, the world around me utterly inaccessible.

This route actually crosses the Colorado River, meeting a route on the other side that ascends to the opposite rim of the Grand Canyon. With river levels as they are these days, it is a guaranteed drowning to cross. In Anasazi time, before dams on the river, it could have been crossed during winter's low water. The route on the other side is the clincher. This had been the perfect access, sewing the Grand Canyon together from east rim to west rim. And how the Anasazi found this, why they would have explored this pit, is difficult to imagine.

I once stopped on a river trip, pulled into a beach across the canyon from here, and found the way up this parallel route, a clean trail of boulders. I remember looking back across the river at the time, not knowing about the Anasazi wormhole route, and thinking, *What pandemonium over there*. It was all caves and arches and broken-down rock, a madhouse of falling cliffs. In fact, a geologist I was with took pictures of this textbook example of collapsing solution pockets burrowed by acidic erosion and bizarre, vermicular erosion.

This was where we were now looking for the way through. Regan stood about sixty feet higher than the rest of us, peering down from a spine of rock. She couldn't see the way either. So we split up, circling the rim of this pit so we could view each other. There was no need to shout. Speaking voices carried easily across the vaults of limestone. We triangulated, directing one person down at a time.

I led Colin. I explained the terrain to him, places he couldn't see. I sent him over a minor ridge, where I told him to go forward and he told me it was a huge exposure. I told him again to go forward and he told me he would die, and suggested that I was not able to see things clearly from my vantage. He crawled back and tried a drainage to his right. Then from the drainage he went out to a ledge.

"I think you're there," I said. "Look ahead of you and down."

"There's the hole."

"Smoke scars on the ceiling?" I asked.

"I can see the smoke scars. It must be the right cave."

Tom, who was watching this maneuver, asked how it looked.

Colin swiveled to see around, sending his arms out as if walking a tightrope. "Well, right where I'm standing is a pretty big exposure, not much to stand on. Then over here, to my side, it drops off, not a lot of room for moving around. Loose rock. A lot of loose rock. Looks like you could stomp and bring this whole thing down, maybe a fall of a hundred feet. And getting to the cave is just more and more of that kind of thing."

Tom chewed on this for a couple seconds. "So, we're talking about fear?"

Colin answered immediately, "Yeah, basically. Fear."

I looked into the pit hoping to see an easier way. There was none. If I had not heard of this route from George, I would have glanced into this place and considered it to be one of those mysteriously unattainable regions. I did not yet have the X-ray eyes that see through solid rock, able to glean these fine, obscure routes. I was learning, though. Already I had walked thousands of miles of canyon country in southern Utah and northern Arizona, hardly ever on an established trail. I studied geology in hopes of understanding the ground. I studied archaeology to get a sense of how people moved across it, looking at their art painted on pieces of pottery. And I studied like this, with my body, my blood quick with fear and expectation. Somewhere, I thought, is the way down. I am looking straight at it, but I cannot see it. I even know where the cave is, and the path eludes me. Somewhere in this race of cliffs is the perfect solution, the land coming down to a single line as artful and precise as a bird feather. We stood in a funnel of a canyon, all of it too sheer to traverse, and below its top rim Colin waited for us in sight of the cave.

We left the bulk of our gear up top, whatever was not necessary, and gathered in Colin's drainage. Once we were collected, we followed him around to the exposure he had found. Progress from there was slow. There was no sense in using ropes with nothing to tie off to. We were physically free. Each person left the safe perch for the descending ledge like astronauts out for a space walk, limbs moving without weight, heads turning slowly. The rocks went. They clattered and fell an unforgiving distance. The small, coconut-sized pieces of limestone shattered on the floor far below us.

Painted pottery sherds from Grand Canyon

The cave turned out to be a good-sized hole in the cliff, tall enough to stand in. When the last person reached its mouth, feet on solid ground, we shook out our fear, ate a little bit of food. Warm air pushed from the entrance, smelling of dust and wood-rat droppings. We shrugged whatever remaining gear we did not need, pulling out the rope and webbing for climbing, headlamps, my note-book. We filed into the darkness, the ceiling above streaked black with smoke scars. It was easy to imagine a procession of Anasazi doing the same, carrying torches of wrapped juniper bark and pine pitch, light-ing their way toward the wormhole.

There were dead and broken stalactites, their slender skins of lime-stone encrusted in dust. Dust everywhere, lifting as we moved, float-ing through our nostrils into our lungs. We walked slowly, quietly, each of us captured by this sensation, the entire landscape becoming a dark, singular passage.

Passageways turned off in numerous directions and we sent our lights into them, taking a few minutes to look around. The correct way was obvious. Back in total darkness was a hole, hardly as wide as my hips. It was a trapdoor in the floor. The rest of the limestone in the cave was sharp and broken, but here, leading into the hole, it was smooth as porce-lain. This was the wormhole George had told us about. The limestone had been long ago burnished by the passage of human skin. We sank our lights into it, but they did not go far. The hole turned sharply from view.

Colin was the first to enter the hole. The only way to fit was to enter feetfirst, body sideways, arms lifted overhead because there was no room for them as his torso passed through. He dropped, his hands the last parts I saw of him. Reports came back up. A panicked voice. "Where does this end?"

He sounded far away.

I stuck my head in. "I don't know. He just said there was a hole."

"I can't see below me. I don't know where this ends. How far does this fall?"

"Feel around."

"Okay, here," he said, relieved, voice coming out of a distant can. "There are ledges to either side. You can catch your feet here to keep from falling."

Regan was the next to enter, slithering into the ground. I thought it ironic, that the Grand Canyon is so immense, and yet this is what it comes to, a hole barely big enough to fit through. It is exactly what George had said: a very simple, beautiful formula for a very complicated expression. All of that hullabaloo of cliffs and boulders and benches that go on forever leads down to this, the perfect answer to the equation. There are no questions left here at the wormhole, just one way down, clear and incontestable.

George once gave to me some of his scientific work published in a journal of mathematics. When I read the material, my eyesight blurred in all of the pages of formulas, letters, numbers, and symbols. The only thing I could decipher was that George's mind was apparently witness to something vast.

The papers were part of what he calls his First Great Epiphany, a mathematical discovery of epic proportion. This was the proving of a series of unconfirmed theorems, the first one being,

$$P\left(R_i \leq b_i,\, 1 \leq i \leq m \mid m,\, n,\, F = G^k\right)$$

$$= \frac{n!}{(n+km)!}\, det\left\{\binom{j}{j-i+1} \frac{\Gamma(\theta_i + kj)}{\theta_i + ki - k}\right\}_{m \times m},$$

Where $\{b_i\}$ is an increasing sequence of integers and $\theta_i = b_i - i + 1$.

I ran my finger across the formula when I saw it, trying to find its intention, seeing only a meaningless jumble. But I knew there was meaning, like the lists of geologic names of the Grand Canyon, enough meaning to bring George fame among his peers worldwide. He spent the next five pages in the journal proving this theorem true with a similar-looking lexicon. To prove something like this true is a breakthrough, revealing a path of logic that has never been utilized, putting the first stroke of human knowledge across the wormhole.

θ is a boulder. $n!$ is a foothold. A theorem is the possibility of a route. Our bodies and our careful moves are the proof. George once took me aside. He told me he'd been thinking about our conversations and my questions about math and route finding. He agreed with me, he said. A route, he told me, is much like a pathway of logic carefully proven true. The confidential language of logic is much like our negotiation of difficult terrain, the way our eyes find ways through what other people might see as dead ends. A person who first proves a theorem is a pioneer. The rest are followers, adding their slickness to the rock.

His First Great Epiphany was succeeded, of course, by what he called his Second Great Epiphany. Instead of math, this epiphany was a passage through a narrow canyon into the Redwall.

I once traveled to his Second Great Epiphany. It was a dark streak of a cleft, a physical struggle. At the entrance to his route I found Anasazi pictographs of humanlike forms and a field of thumbprints dabbed on the wall with ochre and white paint in the shape of a giant abacus. I counted the thumbprints. There were over nine hundred of them. There was also a small, unfired clay figurine resting in a meager shelter nearby. These were markers, proof of the route through here.

Below this ancient artwork, I followed George's epiphany into a narrow hallway. I swam across pools of water and climbed over and to the underside of lodged boulders. I finally gave up in the difficulty of climbs and deep hollows, turning around and climbing out before completing the length of the canyon. But I knew it was a route, that it could be completed had I the skill. George had done it. The Anasazi had done it before him, decorating its entrance as proof.

John dropped into the wormhole, sliding down the tube. It looked as if he was sucked in, gone instantly. Tom followed. I was the last, and I dove feetfirst, following John's example. It shot me through. I twisted into an angle for about five feet and popped out where my boots caught the two opposing ledges. Tom's light came back for me, lifting from below, a searchlight through the fog of dust. If I had kept going, I would have plunged into a toaster slot of a hole that seemed to drop indefinitely. I climbed out of the wormhole's exit into a side chamber where Tom waited.

"They went that way." He pointed off, then dropped to his hands and knees and crawled through a low overhang. I followed, sneaking into the faint blue of daylight where the cave opened again. Old cactus spines pushed through my clothes into my skin, gifts from the wood-rats.

The cave came out at an exposed balcony that hung midway down the cliff of the pit, still a good distance from the floor. I shut off my light and stowed it. Everyone was gathered there, Colin uncoiling the rope. The light was dim, even in the open. Sunlight rarely came directly this far down the canyon. I crouched next to Regan.

"What are we finding?" I asked, reaching to pluck cactus spines from my clothing.

"A long way down still." Her voice was low, as if surgery was taking place in front of us.

This was the way station above the Anasazi stairway. The first rung of the stairs poked out from the balcony like a diving board. It was a single timber inserted into the wall, bolstered with rocks and mortar. Another one protruded not far below and to the left, then another after that. They were too old to be trusted, at least seven hundred years old, probably more around nine hundred. Even if we wanted to use these Anasazi timbers to aid our climb, we could not risk damaging them.

The river was visible from here. We saw it running clear and cold beneath the oval of the arch. We could hear its hiss echoing through the pit. Almost there.

Colin threw the rope down. It snapped as it hit well short of the bottom. "So this is the scary part," he warned us, tugging on his anchor. He had been working as a climbing instructor for Outward Bound, so we each accepted his assessment. None of us wanted to hear this. I peeked off the balcony and saw the fall; bad, loose rock, and the rope hanging in a thin split, a rock chimney, where we would have to climb. The rope would just be a handline. We hadn't brought harnesses or a rappel device, feeling we would not need it. I saw why the Anasazi had built stairs here.

Colin tied in a few hand loops and climbed down, using the rope to steady himself. He groaned, and knocked rocks out. Groaned again, mumbling from gritted teeth. None of us could see him, but we knew what was happening. The rope shivered tight.

He reached a stable level and we could hear him breathing heavily, letting loose the rope. There was only room for one at a time. For half an hour he stayed there. Word was sent up and down, what we could see, what he could see, what none of us could see. He didn't like it. Too much exposure. Overhung. It would be a full commitment to go over the next level, and he did not know if he was ready for such resolution. We didn't have enough rope.

"I don't see a safe way down," Colin finally said. "Maybe it's just that I can't see it from here."

I called to him. "George isn't cavalier about this kind of stuff. He said it could be done without rope if necessary."

"Rope seems pretty necessary for anything I can see from here," Colin said. "Unless you're willing, you know. And I don't know if I'm willing."

Why in the hell were we doing this? To get to the river, then come back up? A free-for-all of primates scrambling down a cliff for no good reason? I leaned back on my haunches. This entire venture suddenly seemed foolish. Half an hour ago I was reveling in this idea of ancient routes narrowing into the Grand Canyon. Now I was thinking we were sent out here by a madman, some romantic, mathematical lunatic. Were we mad, too? I looked over at John. He looked at me. We were thinking the same thing.

Colin called to us. "I'm coming back up."

Time to reassess. If Colin had serious doubts, I trusted them. His body was ideal for this kind of terrain, much like George's, his reach beyond mine. He eventually came crawling out of the chimney to our level.

John said, "Hate to do it, but I'm abandoning ship." It was a brave thing to say.

"Me too," I agreed, not quite as brave, but good enough.

We all exchanged serious looks. John retreated into the cave, followed by Tom, both of them stirring dust and vanishing on their way to the surface. The next one to go was Regan, except she didn't go. She kept looking down.

"What if we can't see the way from here?" she asked.

"That's the problem," Colin reminded her.

"But if it's easy?"

I crawled over to where Colin had anchored the rope and looked down. We had come right up to the edge, the throat of the inner land. I thought of one of George's theorems, a proof he might have abandoned with broken pencil leads and paper scarred by an eraser. But this one was proven. This was not an unexplored route. I looked at Colin and asked, "So is an unfinished route just an unfinished route or is it something in your life left undone?"

Colin's eyes were alert and full of questions. He knew exactly what I meant, exactly what a route is. A pathway, a course, something you could not see or touch, but something that would take you if you were willing. It was the language of this landscape, something so clear that we could read it if we had the right eyes. It would lead us into places beyond the simple reach of our hands and feet. It was being able to see into the rock, finding its transparent planes.

"Definitely something left undone," he answered.

"So this day isn't over?" Regan asked.

Colin shrugged.

At that moment I thought that George Steck was anything but a mad scientist. He was my evidence that what I was doing in this wilderness was not simply the spasms of a misanthrope. I was trying to read the tongue of this land. George is so certain, and so sane, I thought, that if he came here, and if the Anasazi came here before him, I am justified. I want to see how far this earth will take me.

"I'm going down," I said.

Colin, his eyes still sharp, nodded. Regan nodded too. I went.

The chimney ran for maybe twenty feet, a direct downward line to the next ledge, not much of a ledge. My fingers dug and searched over the rock, holding my full weight. The rope helped, wrapped into my right hand, passed off to my left as I renegotiated. There was fear. I could smell it off my skin and in my breath. Loose rocks shot out, clattering against each other, followed by the silent free-fall and the burst of impact. Using the rope, I swung across to a good ledge. The sound of the river below was so pleasing. Again, we were almost there. The amount of time it took for a fallen rock to hit the floor was becoming less and less.

"I'm down where you were, Colin," I called up.

"Do you see the problem I had, the commitment you'd have to take?"

"I see it. Just like you said."

"Overhung?"

"Completely overhung. I don't see a way. But George said it was here."

Regan's voice came in. "What about behind you?"

I looked behind me at a wedge of rock a little lower. I imagined stretching my body to reach it and could feel how my balance would move away from the wall and into space. The center of my gravity would have to aim exactly down to that wedge, stopped by a single boot tip. It would be a fall into the air just to get there, a motion of utter faith. But it had been done. It was out of reach of the wooden ladder remains, so I knew that the Anasazi had done it by climbing bare-handed.

I said, "You would have to get to it, this little foothold down there. Looks solid, though. Colin?" My voice was searching for support.

Colin heard my tone, a trick we've long played with each other, sending confidence back and forth, as firm and helpful as an outstretched hand. "I'll come down," he said.

Within ten minutes each of the three of us—Colin, Regan, and I—had taken the step, one at a time, sending our bodies over the edge and catching ourselves on a little snap of rock. We were all three out on the face, talking back and forth, short words, encouragement and warnings. Tom and John had reached the next rim up and were shouting encouragement down to us. They looked small and sounded far away.

The commitment took us into a beautiful line of holds, and suddenly the rock wall revealed itself. It was a sheet of math. Symbols and digits ran across the face in faultless order, each one stepping to the next, as if it had been left by hand. The only hand here was erosion, ticks and snaps out of the rock, bulges in the right places. Every hold came at a perfect pace, easily within reach and I stretched ahead, towing myself across, knowing exactly why the Anasazi had come here. There was no danger to this final climb. We each came down out of breath, grinning in disbelief. I thought of George's wonderful formulas as I stopped on level ground and looked back up. We had spoken with this quiet wall, finding its language, and it fanned above me, what could have been random crags and crevices, but were instead a way of living.

At the floor of the canyon we walked among boulders, entering the passage of the arch. Directly below the arch the limestone gave us one last drop. The entire canyon narrowed to a bluish passageway, a thread of a drainage that fell straight down to the river. We were there, almost able to touch the water. Colin climbed into the final descent. When he said, "Oh shit," I made my decision. "Not that bad," he smiled up to me. "I mean, if we went back and pulled the rope down, which I think we could do now, we could get down this no problem. We could even do it without the rope."

I sighed, making sure he heard me.

"Why don't you come down and see what you think, just try it out," he offered.

So I did. We switched places, him climbing out, me climbing in. I got down to where I was hanging over about twenty-five feet down to the river. A boulder was stuck in behind me, over my head. He was right. It looked possible, but not too possible. The river in front of us sailed by clear and swift. I could see the beach where I had once landed in a wooden dory, and the first limestone ledges that start the route up the other side.

At this point the last feet were not so important to me, not worth the hazard. This was the floor of the canyon for me. It was the completion of the route. I sat there jammed in the end of the canyon for a couple of minutes, the limestone cold on my shoulders. Regan scrambled around the upper ledges, exploring the upward slopes of the arch, shouting out discoveries and beautiful things now and then. She had no interest in playing this boy's game of getting to the river and beating on our chests. She knew better. She wanted to get back up to her pack alive, happy, and hungry. When Colin standing above me gave a look, wanting to know if I had any interest in going farther, risking my ass to get to the river, I said, "I'm done."

Like a rock thrown down a crevice, I had dropped through hole after hole until wedging here. The path taken was the math of an ardent landscape. It is what I believed I would find, proof. There is a way through this place, intricate as machinery, as concealed as secrecy.

In two days, when we returned to George on the highest rim, he had one question. The answer would tell the entire story, giving him everything he needed to know about our journey.

Did you find it?

Yes, we found it.

LABYRINTH

Southern Utah

The middle of December, a week away from the frigid solstice. A pot of snow on my stove. I settled over it, reducing it to drinking water liberally dusted with blow-sand and tiny kernels of rock. Two of us had set our camp in the open, unprotected on a sandstone spine arcing above a thicket of canyons. The region surrounding us was an isolated and furious storm, a place where the stone earth has heaved itself upward, opening innumerable crevasses burdened under layers of shadow. We came up to this high point to capture the last prized light of day.

My partner, a tall, early-thirties man named Devin Vaughan, hunted below a cluster of stunted junipers like a mouse preparing for winter, gathering handfuls of dry sticks and old, papery grass stems to burn.

Devin is a river outfitter and engine mechanic from Moab, Utah, a frequent companion of mine on long walks. He is an attractive man, his face sharply featured, a small and narrow mouth and a steeply cut jawline. He is one of only four people I know who have enough intimacy with this place to navigate it end to end. He carries a map with him, taped at the rips and folds, worn soft and jotted on with a pen. He marks every successful route in red. His map's topographic features are as convoluted as a brain, and within them his red lines backtrack and overlap in a way that suggests lunacy.

Little more than ten miles long and five miles wide, this is a confined and arid maze of canyons. Hordes of faults and fractures break through the terrain, dividing the basement rock into thin upright bands. Hundreds of these fins run alongside each other like salmon teeming up a shallow river. Between are plunging unlit banks of boulders and windless glens. The east side is shielded by a twelve-hundred-foot cliff; its northern boundary a nearly impenetrable field of sandstone risers; and to the south and west is a lengthy, straight-walled canyon that cups the region like a hand. Within these protective outer walls is this island of dissected rock where we finally ended our tasks and stood to watch the sun clip beneath the horizon.

Out there, ahead of us in this darkening, perplexing land was our destination. In the center of this labyrinth the fins spread like an opening lotus, wings of stone falling back to reveal the single soul of nowhere. It is a snake carved into the rock, left by the Anasazi maybe nine hundred years ago. Thirty feet long, nearly as wide as a spread hand, this snake sweeps horizontally across the foot of a cliff, its body rippling with motion. Like pilgrims, we had come to this snake numerous times in the past, approaching it along routes from the east, west, and north. This winter we were searching for a new route, starting at the south end of this maze and attempting a northward crossing.

I would have tried this passage with no one other than Devin. His physical movements in rough country are so cultivated and graceful they seem to rhyme. I have seen him fly, sailing into the air, reflecting off a wall to grab a handhold on the other side. He is a fine route finder, perhaps the best I have ever met. The way he sees the landscape's code heartens me, his eyes luring pathways from impossible places. The planet opens to him.

This time of year every night is colder and darker than the last, our bodies a bit slower, more conservative in the chill. We each had a small fire pan. We fed them twigs and pulls of dry grass. As we huddled over our flickers of warmth, we said little, busy adding sticks and rearranging our fires.

"Tomorrow," he said, turning the word up into a question. "Move due north from here?"

I poked the fire around in my pan to keep the smoke down, my face held directly over the flames. "North," I agreed.

In the morning north sent us a little west and east, then south again. We kept our gear light. Neither of us carried a tent. Too heavy. We melted snow when needed, keeping the weight off of our backs. Climbing into crossword puzzles of fissures, we removed our packs from time to time, hoisting them to each other. The rock formations passing around us were as elegant as ear bones, great overhead arches and fine lips of handholds.

We climbed into a sandstone cleft, a place where water once ran. Ahead it dropped into darkness, out of sight. A juniper tree had fallen and was jammed, its pewter-colored wood old and splintered. It had been here for some time. We left our packs on a ledge, heading down to explore this space, seeing if it was a way of travel or not.

Devin tied a length of climbing webbing to his waist while I tied the other end to mine. If he fell, my body would catch behind him like the wedged tree. Professional climbers might scoff at our quick and rudimentary techniques, but this is the way to move here, throwing a bowline around our bodies several times a day as a quick backup. We both wore gloves with the fingertips cut off. Day gloves. The fleece had worn so thin in places that the lines in our knuckles were visible. He ventured farther into the crack, using his shoulders and back to hold himself, sending a hand flat against the wall as a brace. Dislodging a rock with his boot, he kicked it free to test the depth of the passage below him.

It clacked and rattled as if dropped down a well. We leaned over to listen. It fell at least a hundred feet. What we could not see below us suddenly became huge, like the throat of an unimaginable beast.

"No, no, no," Devin said, turning around quickly. "This isn't the way."

I agreed, reeling him back on the webbing.

Devin had been studying this region for ten years, poking his way through a place not much larger than the town in which he lived, and had still not deciphered even half of its routes. This hugeness inside of smallness creates a matrix of intersections, precious and incalculable channels one after the next. It is a fractal landscape like the surface of a leaf, veins within veins, or the arborescent feathers of ice forming barbs inside of barbs across the surface of a pond.

I had to find a way of keeping track, looking behind me to consider the terrain I had just come through, ledges slick with ice skirting a small plunge above where Devin and I had retreated with our webbing, then beyond that a stone-walled avenue where juniper trees grow along the bottom. It was not an option for me to memorize all of this in order to find my way back in case this route did not go. There were too many turns and decisions. I had to instead remember by allowing myself to remain in each passageway after I had gone. I made a ceaseless inquiry of the place, not asking questions as I walked, but rather presenting myself openly, taking in the environment without governing the incoming information. I did not deal in unnecessary thoughts, concerns about tonight's meal or tiredness in my legs. I walked slowly, brushing my gloved hands on walls, pausing atop high fins, my head filled with imagery and no words.

I left a skein of my presence throughout this maze, strands of sensations that might lead me back, that would be with me days from now, likely decades from now, because they were not sensations restricted to my eyes or my tongue. Everything I came across entered me like a dream. I was turning my life into twine, stretching myself through these corridors until my body was only a mark along the way. Otherwise, I would find myself suddenly lost, turning quickly, not knowing the direction to or from.

But always the snake lay in my mind like a compass point. I was aware as I turned how it was now at my back, then to my side, with days of baffling, unknown topography between here and there.

Devin had first brought me to the snake a few years earlier during the height of summer. We had arrived exhausted, heat shimmering off our skin. I held my eyes up to see the single piece of art, tracing its curved outline along the wall. I had swayed slowly in the heat below it. Dredging deep into my body for any word that might fit, I said, "*Snake . . . yes . . . hot . . . shade?*"

Its interior is pointillist, filled with hundreds of small peck marks that are crowded, but not overlapped. The head is eye-shaped, wide at the jaw and pointed at the tip. The body stretches from right to left with supple curves, the crests and troughs forming perfect symmetry. I had thought upon first seeing it that this snake describes how a person must live and travel here: find the sweet and elegant course that lies within this turmoil; understand the patterns concealed in the land; walk unfettered through the maze. This is the reward for knowing the way through, this snake waiting in the center where the earth unfolds.

As we traveled north this winter we crossed numerous broad openings that appeared at the meeting places of canyons and joints within the sandstone. We came on each of these interior regions surprised, clambering through a crease to suddenly arrive at open sunlight. These were gardens hanging in the chaos, juniper trees and tight clumps of blackbrush finding purchase in sand. Everything was cold and silent in these open places. We ran into the basins shouting, kicking through the sand. Our bodies opened like horses let out at full gallop. Fifty seconds across stood the opposite wall, honeycombed with minor canyon mouths and boulders where we had to slow ourselves and concentrate, finding the way out again.

For the sake of knowing where we were or where we had been, we used these basins as reference points, calling them First or Second Land. Fourth Land, Sixth Land, whichever. In the Seventh Land we stopped to rest. Devin walked slowly, examining the ground.

"What do you see?" I called.

He looked up as if puzzled to hear me. He walked over. "I haven't seen any bighorn tracks. No coyotes or mountain lions. No large animals."

I had not seen them either. In this sort of desert we would expect to at least find the lobed pads of coyote tracks, or the praying hands of bighorn prints, but not here. Like listening to the rock tumbling down the crack earlier, this information about animals suddenly revealed a gulping acquaintance. *A place where even animals can't reach,* I thought.

It was like walking in a dungeon down here, the walls cold and half-lit. A faint mist of breath drifted around us, coiling against the rock. The passage rounded out, womblike. The walls above came close enough together that rocks the size of soccer balls were caught over our heads and we passed beneath, cautiously, curiously glancing up.

Devin found water and called me over. In the crotch of a small, declivitous side canyon was a frozen pool. This was good news. No more sand in our water. He picked up a rock and with a few well-delivered blows, broke through. Slabs of ice buckled and floated. We both removed gloves and submerged our bottles, plunging our already cold hands into the water.

Devin's left hand came out bright pink. Grinning, he looked up and asked, "Does the desert always provide?"

I pulled out my own hand, the skin taut and alive with cold.

We camped that night in this hole of a canyon. Theatrical light from our single campfire broke up through the walls, casting eerie shadows two hundred feet over our heads. The view of the stars was through a single opening where the walls spread like bread dough pulled apart, wedged rocks still joining the two sides. When the fire burned down we could see the stars more clearly, a luminescent trail of overhead dust.

"We need a better view of the sky," I said, standing up from the coals.

Devin followed me with his eyes. Then he looked up to see the stars and back to me. He made a grunting sound of approval, lifting his folds of clothing to a standing position.

Our boots crunched through snow as we left. We walked down the canyon to where it fell open, the walls backing apart. The stone beneath us slid a hundred feet into the throat of a canyon, coatings of ice sloping along it. In front of us the western quadrant of stars came into full view. We stood at this edge as if we had both been presented to the sky, held forward in palms of sandstone.

We were quiet for some time. We listened. There was no wind, no sound. The stars were each clear, not so much lights as they were points of contact. It is said that there are only six thousand stars visible to the eye, but tonight there were more. They fell back from nearest and highest of magnitude to those so faint or distant that they turned to powder, and from powder to a thin brume.

The lines I had been laying of myself across the ground reached upward. I found myself oriented by stars, by constellations and gas clouds where swaths of stars were entirely hidden. I had been out for enough nights over the past years that I came to distinguish suggestive patterns among even the dimmer stars. I had recognized to within a number of days when Mars or Jupiter had gone into retrograde motion and begun slowly backtracking across the sky. There were routes among the stars that were as effective and methodical as those I found on the ground. In the map Devin and I were attempting to create here, the sky held weight equal to the earth, especially in winter.

"Good stars," I finally said.

"Good stars," he replied softly. "This is why we come to the ass end of nowhere. Stars like this."

There is a sameness between Devin and me. We see this same horrible violence, cliffs collapsing and frozen, these stars held as if about to burst. We see this hugeness, leaving the electric lights behind, the vibrancy of humanity, to enter the dark turns of rock, looking for only these things: process, comprehension, stone, a rope dangling for a way out. The stars were what we looked for tonight. We both saw the sky spreading into paths of insoluble order. The stars moved, winking out one by one as the horizon lifted against them.

There are three ways I know of to record the turning of the heavens. Mechanical equipment, such as time exposures on a camera, will show streaks of motion, every careening circle of light fixed around a single motionless star in the north, Polaris. Another way to see different star patterns come and go for each season is to stay out across winters like we were doing, moving wherever necessary to view the sky each night, protected by warm clothes, skin on your face cold as glass. The third way to understand the sky is through the Anasazi snake carved in the center of this maze.

The snake was still an unknown number of days away, but I thought about it often during our approach. It is the Polaris around which the desert seasons turn. One of the people who knows the way through here, a friend named R.T., once made a discovery that changed our impression of the snake, defining it not only as an earth-bound subject, but also as one of the sky. R.T. had come in from a westward route during the summer solstice, the longest day of the year, and sat in front of the snake as the morning sun first crossed it. At that moment the sunlight fell through a crack above and to the west, casting a single beam onto the head of the snake. It was an arrowhead of light, fully articulated, pointing down, narrowing and then expanding to make a hafted butt where it should be tied to an arrow shaft. The image lasted less than thirty seconds. The head of the snake, he realized, had been placed here to briefly hold this arrowhead of solstice light.

I came out once, working through the flat heat of June for the summer solstice to witness R.T.'s discovery. In the morning I had waited in front of the snake, its body curving up and down to the simple harmony of a sine wave. The first sunlight to come through a nearby crevice formed a dagger on the head. No light landed anywhere else. The dagger quickly spread. In a matter of seconds, synchronized to the movement of the sun, light shaped into an arrowhead over the snake's head.

The arrowhead was faultlessly defined for that moment. The ground and the sky became seamless, a single sphere. Just when the arrowhead was tangible, the light continued outward, leaking across the wall. The sphere of sky and earth divided, returning to their two places.

What I had seen was unmistakable. It was an astronomical calculation. A year of waiting culminated in the momentary crossing of shadow, light, and artifact. The Southwest is riddled with such alignments, huge kivas drawing light onto altars and niches to mark each shift of season, deviant lunar cycles pouring through slots onto stone-faced petroglyphs. This entire canyon desert, with its countless sundial grooves, gouges, and nocks, is a massive calendar, a place bound to the sky.

Standing this night on the edge beside Devin, I was certain that it did not take the Anasazi long to discover these parallels in the sky and to marvel at their connections here on earth. They took note of changing seasons, and saw on the ground shadows extending and falling back, markings all around as if they had been living in a mansion of pillars and shadows. There is nothing for me that offers as much comfort and invincibility as the night sky, yet Anasazi knowledge goes beyond mine by hundreds of centuries. The certainty and mastery that they witnessed in the sky must have been unbearable.

The first sunlight came through a small crescent canyon ahead of me. It reached across the floor and beamed onto the opposite wall. Carrying a smaller pack for the day, I walked over to it, placing my body in the path. I lit up like a rising ghost. Even now, by first light, I was tired. My mind had been worn bare with travel. Handholds had been sometimes too small to see and snow had stolen my traction across the inclines. When I moved, my eyes were tight, alert only to the handhold, the step, the rock. Traveling through this country in winter required the single-minded instincts of dogs.

Devin was walking somewhere up ahead, beyond the sunlight, maybe even in another canyon by now, as we scouted the next leg of our route. Coming out of blank walls where I failed at my own course, I scanned for his footprints to follow: a thin plate of rock broken by a boot step, a misplaced twig, or a scuff in the snow. His tracks led me up spindles of sandstone that I would never have sought on my own, only strengthening my conviction that he was the most polished route finder I had known. Why would he have come up here? Always there was a reason, a nearby course, or a view to the correct way.

I never mentioned to him the times I felt completely lost, my memory of choices, turns, abandoned routes, and narrow passageways becoming confusion, my string stretched too tight, snapping so that entire reaches I had walked returned to the unknown. He was not having the same difficulty. His engineering mind saw into this land the way I looked at the sky: here is irresistible order.

I tracked behind him, climbing apprehensively through steep hatchways between boulders, tearing my clothes in the friction. His prints hugged me along a ledge up to a high tip of sandstone. I stopped there over the swarming darkness of canyons below. We were today trying to form a circle through the fins and canyons, another path for Devin's map. In this, we were finding the next leg to reach the snake, leaving our full packs in camp to be returned to tonight.

I looked over the terrain, hunting for Devin and perhaps the next route. I thought of two men who recently drove to a canyon that skirts the far north end of this place. They parked a sport utility vehicle as far in as was possible, then walked for a three-hour tour. Curious about the convoluted land farther south, they kept going.

Three days later someone in a valley beyond here saw them flailing their arms against the horizon atop an eastern border of cliffs. That evening water was dropped to them, literally dropped, wrapped in sleeping bags and tossed from a helicopter. The next day a search and rescue team abandoned an attempt to reach them from the ground. No one on the team knew how to get there, and then how to get out. An airlift was finally called and the men were plucked safely from this labyrinth.

Not far from where they had left their vehicle is the northern entrance into here. They had found the way in, but once inside, stone fins wrapped around them, spinning their minds. Canyons lapped over canyons. They could not even remember which direction was at their backs. At this same northern entrance is a marquee of Anasazi petroglyphs that the two men likely did not see. There is one that could have helped them, offering a warning about what they were about to enter. This petroglyph is of a spiral-like loop of passages nested into each other, carved into red stone. Some of the passages are dead ends, while others go off for long redundant curves dividing and rejoining. Just below this maze petroglyph, inches away, stands a small person carved into the rock. The person is poised at the edge, as if waiting to go in.

Maze petroglyph

I have stopped at this person-and-maze petroglyph a number of times. The human figure stands facing forward, an empty circle forming its head. The figure expresses exactly the sensation of standing at the northern perimeter, preparing to enter, the feeling of a gap about to be bridged, hovering at the edge of the mystery.

I was now far inside, the person within the maze aiming for its center. From my spire-top in the low midday sun of December I noticed my shadow against a nearby cliff. Another human shadow appeared beside mine and I quickly turned. Devin stood on the next knob of rock, thirty feet away.

He squatted to make himself comfortable and pointed outward, tracing something in the air with a finger emerging from his cut-off glove. "Look down around there."

I followed his finger. Indeed, one of the fins had a spine rising shallowly enough that it could be climbed, up and over its arc down into a field of canyons. It was exactly the direction we needed to be heading.

"I see it," I said.

In the northern distance I could make out familiar sets of fins that housed the snake. We had to travel west first, then back to the east before meeting another route to the north. The snake was still a few days away.

Devin looked over to me. He gestured loosely with his arm, covering the whole of the landscape below us. "How long do you think we can be pummeled, I mean seeing stuff like this and still be able to return and function in the other world?"

"It's too late," I said.

He laughed loudly, standing. "Yes. Too late." He pounced off his point of rock, landing on a ledge to the other side. I turned to watch him go. I was tired, not ready to walk again. But I didn't want him too far ahead. I thought I might never be seen again if I was left alone in here.

I looked in the direction of our camp, trying to see a route. For the rest of the day we would be crossing collisions of geology, huge landforms heaved together then divided into smooth faces. I reluctantly climbed down from my perch to follow Devin.

An hour later we arrived at the fin he had pointed out. It was like climbing the back of the St. Louis Arch with a little extra leeway of friction and incline. There was no place for rope or any kind of protection other than our bodies and bald rock. Devin scrambled ahead of me moving hand by hand, relying on momentum and swift thought.

The back of the fin was no more than a foot or two wide, dropping fifty feet down either side, then one hundred feet, then one hundred fifty feet. I kept a good pace, burning my climbing muscles as my mind worked rapidly pulling interior fuses and wires, disconnecting fear. The drop yawned around me. Fear rose like bile, stinging the inside of my throat.

I focused on my hands, my fingers, keeping the surrounding drop to a vibrating blur. But the blur became crisper than even my hands in front of me. I could see at the edges of my eyes huge boulders that from here looked small, exactly where I would land if I fell. I imagined falling. A slip of the hand. My left foot landing a quarter-inch in the wrong direction. I suddenly froze.

In a flush of conflicting instinct, I clamped my body against the narrow dorsum of sandstone, like clutching a metal pole. My lips met the cold grain and I huffed a hard breath against it. My eyelashes brushed the rock. No. This was wrong. A perfect ascent was broken. Momentum lost, I would not be able to find traction again. Fear saturated my blood. I barely adhered to the nearly sheer rock, my muscles beginning to shake.

Devin topped the fin, arriving at a safe foothold. He turned and when he saw me straight below him, panic streaked through his eyes. "Crap," he blurted. "Don't do this."

"Already did it," I said. I shot a look below me, over my left shoulder, then up to Devin again.

He also released an anxious breath, studying my position.

My voice was angry and strained. "I lost my faith," I said.

He understood exactly what I meant. There is nothing more erosive. He could not reach me to offer help without putting himself in the same peril. He chewed on his thoughts for a moment, looking at my options from nearly overhead.

"I'll keep moving," he said, his tone resolved. "You don't need me here." He turned and I listened to him climb away.

Then I hung there alone. I admired him for that instant, how quickly he could make the correct decision and make it happen.

Faith was the one gem that I had in my life, seated deep inside of my body. It was a devotion to process and form—faith that every move leads to the next. Now I was paralyzed on the curve of a rock. I closed my eyes, cooling my blood.

I practiced breathing, listening to my heartbeat tapping from inside. I opened my eyes. The texture against my body was full of tiny grains, good sandstone. I remembered how well I knew this peach-colored formation, how it would respond to boots and hands at different grades.

I looked up once. There was no way to go higher and I assured myself of this. Down, there was a pale foothold about eight feet below me. It was a ledge protruding by no more than half of an inch, enough to hold my weight. Reaching it could only be done by falling. From there I could climb down.

But the fear came back, barging drunkenly into my head, knocking things over. My fingers tightened against the rock. I closed my eyes again. *This will not do,* I thought. *I have to be solid.* So I went ahead and killed myself. I got rid of my mind, smashing it into the rock. It was a swift act. Once that was out of the way, I opened my eyes again and took a second to review the next eight feet below me.

I removed my hands from the rock and fell.

My body scraped down the pitch, shirt and pants rasping loudly. Hands scrambled from nick to nick, touching just long enough to brake for a quarter-second, a sixteenth of a second. As speed increased, flesh skidded from my fingers. I pointed my boot tips into the wall. Just above the ledge I delivered all my weight to them. I caught the ledge, taking the impact with my knees. My upper body swayed out for an instant on the very toe of my boots, the impact wanting to carry me farther. Then I came back to the rock face.

I took a few seconds to breathe, settling my heart rate. I moved a foot down, then a hand. When I reached the base of the fin a few minutes later, I shook my arms out. My muscles quaked. The fear and strain in my blood tasted hot. I remembered what Devin had told me the first time he saw this land of fins ten years earlier. "It's one of those places where if I want to understand it," he had told me, "it'll need to become a religion."

A religion, I thought, looking back up at the fin. Then, I am baptized. I picked sand out of the abrasions in my fingertips and walked off to find another way.

On the seventh day we had our camp in the high eastern region. Below and to all sides were hundreds of stone temples standing shoulder to shoulder. Snow graced each northern flank. We gathered twigs at the end of the day and once again pulled on our warmest clothing. Wind trafficked through the spaces below us, sending up hissing tones of conversations.

The sun touched the southwest horizon. We stopped whatever we were doing and faced it.

"Every night we go through this," Devin said without breaking eye contact with the sunset. "Everything's going to be different here. In thirty seconds."

I nodded and said nothing. My face was strangely warm in this final, brassy glow. The very surface was nipped cold, but I felt the heat underneath, at my bones.

As the sun shrank, the light turned tepid. Devin pointed straight at the bright, sinking knob, saying, "Watch it. It doesn't even pause. This whole thing is wound around us, some kind of great machine that's about to close us out. There it goes. There . . . there . . ." He inhaled when it happened. The light flashed out.

"Done," he said. He turned to me. His voice was softer now, a little crazy. "Now, here we are."

On these winter days, once the sun is gone, the world changes. Whatever we were in the sunlight, we ceased and became something different in the dark, from mobile, animated creatures to cold, huddled rocks.

A deep violet color poured overhead. We got around to our two small fires in their pans, stoking them as we sat near each other. We blew into the mounds of coals, carefully adding twigs and arranging them as if building a ship in a bottle. The fires rose and fell as we kept them fed. The snake was now a short distance away. Neither of us had seen it during the winter solstice. Tomorrow we would go.

In the stranded hours of darkness I thought of a man I know, an astrophysicist named Kim Malville. He would enjoy this artifact that we were about to reach, I thought. I had studied under him as an undergraduate at the University of Colorado, and tonight I remembered how his talk used to be filled with terms that mystified me: *the houses of the sun, symbolic geometry, sacred mandalas.* He saw ceremony everywhere, and it is perhaps from him that I learned to watch for it. Together we sank into hours of conversation, pushing at the edges of science like excitable children. It enchanted me to see an older man weathered and lithe, his eyes alert to every thought. Once in a planetarium he stood at the controls spinning stars over my head as fast as he could move them, changing the positions to take us back thousands of years. He was laughing like a madman the whole time.

Adding to his role as an astrophysicist, he took a strong, professional interest in archaeoastronomy, drawing the stars down to earth, back to the people who had lived here. A few years back he discovered in the Saharan Desert astronomically aligned stone monoliths and a small circle of upright slabs. The alignments consisted of stones, some weighing two tons; most of the stones were buried in the sand. He found six major alignments extending across the sediments of a dry lake for about a third of a mile. Predating Stonehenge by two thousand years, this site became the oldest known megalithic archaeoastronomical site in the world, dating to 5000 B.C. This knowledge of the sky, he taught me, is as old as the human mind. He had found lifted stone monoliths near the Utah–Colorado border, placed, he imagined, to cast shadows marking certain celestial events. That site, around which thirty thousand Anasazi once lived, may well have been thought of as the center of the universe, considering the way events in the sky are lined up with dominant local landmarks.

He fed my curiosity when I studied with him. He told me of excavations where he had worked, finding astronomical alignments with artifacts that were accurate down to halves of degrees, using transect equipment just to make sure of it. I imagined him in the field the same way he was manning the planetarium, his eyes dazzled with whirling patterns.

At the top of the fins tonight I worked my fire down to coals thinking of Kim Malville and his ravishing universe. It was above my head right now, the dark, consuming hand of the sky. Sitting cross-legged in front of my coals, I kept my face close, blowing into them, my skin warming at each bright pulse. Devin did the same, shoving coals around with his last stick. Finally it was over. The coals were no longer worth it. I had kept my attention on the ground for a couple of hours, never allowing myself a long upward stare. The pleasures of the night needed to be judiciously divided, otherwise the cold would become insufferable.

I sat with my back straight, my head turning up to see the stars. We had the full view from here, stars down to every horizon. Devin and I sat as quietly as possible, the glow reducing beneath us as the world turned from the real into the unreal. Infinite space extended over us. I felt the curve of the planet, how it faced into this celestial landscape, a giant orb of rock suspended among stars, floating because it could not fall. There was no place to fall to. It left a queer sensation, bolts of panic and ecstasy. The threads of my life spread across a landscape of light years, from this desert through the stars and back. My body was too small to possibly contain this.

How long, indeed, until we were pummeled? The sunlight hours gave us the earth—the fins, canyons, and lopsided boulders. These long nights were nothing but sky, a radiant and deep color that could not possibly have a name, the earth gone from us. Tomorrow it would return, tearing like an animal at our clothes.

Tomorrow we would go to the snake and step into the winter align-ment between this earth and this sky.

I left in the morning long before the sun. Stars bathed my movements. Devin was still in his bag. He would catch up later. I walked west, aiming toward the red-eyed star of Orion. It began setting over the far cliffs as I dropped through the first leading canyons.

The land came visible under a thin, watery light. I could barely see fins rising ahead of me, sequential outlines that were the secret to knowing how to navigate this place. I walked a memory of benches and small back-tracks from years of travel to the snake, a cut between walls that dropped one after the next, a huge staircase leading through a notch into a basin. A falling star streaked into the southern sky, breaking into a shower of pieces before dissolving, flushing into a green line, never allowed to touch ground. The eastern sky held the final cut of a crescent moon, almost a new moon. In every object around me, in the sky and on the earth, I saw this calendar. The universe seemed poised, each item in perfect place.

The moon was the most glaring of these items for the moment. Clear as a Cheshire grin, it hovered low in the sky, sickle thin. Every day and night the moon rises in a different place at a different time, then every month it is somewhere else again. Among the idyllic cycles of the sun and seasons, the moon is an alluring nemesis. It crosses at unorthodox angles, swinging drunkenly over the horizons.

Fancifully, I thought of the nearby snake as a solar and lunar balance.

It has the sun's bearing, but with the moon's data. The length of its body bears six troughs and seven crests, adding up to thirteen, the number of new moons in the year. Within the confines of a solar year, the moon gets abridged, allowed to complete only twelve and a half of its own cycles, which causes a disparity between moon time and sun time. At the snake, lunar phases could be counted starting at the summer solstice arrowhead. Working down the snake's body, every trough and crest would be marked by each month of the moon. The last moon of the lunar cycle would land in the final trough of the snake's tail, exactly one solar year after the moon-counting began, the moment that the next arrowhead of sunlight touches the head of the snake, the moment to begin counting again. Calendars for the moon and the sun would balance out across this snake.

As I walked, twilight met the moon above the horizon and began washing it away. I dropped from view of both Orion and the fading moon, winding toward a broad opening between fins. Crossing this clearing, I heard a raven coming through, its wings flapping hard against the cold. I stopped to watch it pass. Up the other side, I scrambled through house-sized boulders that formed a steep three-hundred-foot apron below a cliff. As I came to the foot of the cliff I saw the snake within arm's reach of the ground. I stopped there, letting my heart slow from the climb. My eyes moved across the entire plane of the cliff, and I could not bring them back to the snake for at least another minute, taking in the angles of rock and the distances around me.

The snake is always a startling find, even knowing it is here, like coming across a Picasso painting lying on its side in an alley. It is literally in the middle of nowhere, boulders unfolded randomly beneath it. The horizontal body carries a sensuous tension flexing thirty feet from head to tail. It had been chiseled into the flesh of deep red sandstone, revealing the much paler rock within. When I came closer I stopped again and lifted my gloved hand in the air, tracing its ophidian crests and troughs. Curves spent themselves across the wall like water.

If you sat in the desert for a year with a clock and a Gregorian calendar, you would find that your time does not match what you see in the world around you. The snake, the stars, the sun, and the moon belong to an interlocking design. We fool ourselves with our inventions. The gears of true time are not round like those of the clock. The earth travels at different speeds during different times of the year, slinging faster and slower around the sun, making European winters eight days shorter than those in Australia. Lunar and solar cycles set up a complex rhythm obeying doublets and triplets, not the singular boxes of weekdays and months. We are made to look like simpletons the way we spoon-feed ourselves with our artless time of minutes, hours, and days, leap years thrown in to jury-rig our twelve months so that they don't fall into disrepair. We add and subtract sixty minutes of daylight saving time to our seasons to make our workdays more efficient, our heads buried in business while around us these flawless patterns pass like the hand of God.

I kept still in the cold, waiting in this place where true time shows itself. Soon the sun arrived. Light soaked each high point of stone hundreds of feet above. Shadows slid back into their crevices. Breezes came up as the cold sink of morning lazily rolled over itself. When the sun touched the head of the snake, it was nothing like summer solstice. Summer light had been pure white. This was the molten color of red curry. Instead of a discrete arrowhead, now came a two-hundred-foot wave of light. Absolutely vertical, it spanned the height of the cliff like an opening theater curtain.

Every tie that I had to the night sky came to me. This was the convergence of unimaginably expansive spheres—the inviolable sky, and the forged land. The snake had been slipped into place, a knot binding the two. I stood at the meeting point as these forces silently crossed each other like galaxies sliding together, and then apart.

When the sun finally moved beyond the snake's tail, warming the rock face until I felt it on my skin, I heard a peculiar, metallic sound. It twanged musically far in the distance, barely audible. I turned from the snake and looked out. The thing, whatever it was, plucked rhythmically. Perplexed, I traced the sound to a high notch I had come through earlier. There, Devin sat against a boulder playing a Jew's harp, snapping the metal tong against his open mouth. He was at my eye level a mile away. How long had he been there? Had he watched the light come across the snake?

I found a place to sit in the boulders, resting in the warmth of my clothes and the new sun. I listened to Devin's performance. With all of this fantastic consequence swirling around me, holy alignments striking down everywhere, Devin was a strange Puck in the rocks. Humans, I thought, what fantastic creatures we are, spinning like dervishes in these forever domains of star paths and canyons, grasping the extent of this landscape in one moment, forgetting in another. We lay out maps for ourselves as if we cannot see clearly enough with our own eyes. At the same time we expand beyond the farthest edges of our girded maps. We are perfect for this place. Never still and never simple.

TOWERS

Southeast Utah

In the long nights of winter I practiced dying. Motionless in my bag I prepared myself so that I wouldn't leave a ghost when I went. I slowed my breathing. My mind turned quiet, not engaging in its constant rhetoric. I unwrapped my heart, pulling back layers of gauze-like fabric until there was nothing left of me. Then I turned my eyes and looked at the emptiness that had been me. This endeavor helped send me back to sleep on the tenth or eleventh hour after nightfall.

I was dead, ghostless, when I breathed snow into my lungs and woke. Snow swept in like lace curtains at an open window. The air was cold enough that I didn't leap out naked and haul myself and my bag off to shelter under an overhang or into the shadow of a juniper tree.

I just closed the entrance to the bag so I would stop inhaling snow in my sleep. I tucked my head and listened to the pulsing rattle of winter on nylon.

It was not warm enough for snow to melt and soak in. In the morning it would shake off easily as flour. I was awake now. My breath warmed my face. Four in the morning, midnight, hard to tell. I had been asleep for hours, awake for hours, asleep again. The last ten nights had been this way as I traveled across southeast Utah on another trek with Devin Vaughan, retreating into my bag for twelve, thirteen hours each night. It was too cold to be out waiting for dawn.

The wind outside kept inching into my night thoughts. The hissing sound of gusts and snow rose and fell across my sleeping bag. Cold leaked through with each strong push. I curled tighter. Devin lay fifteen feet away in the lee of a cliff wall. He was awake, had to be. The wind was coming strong. The snow sounded hard, like sand.

While I listened to the wind, dreams came from nowhere. I fell asleep without knowing it. How long this lasted, I couldn't say, but when I woke next, the snow had stopped. I opened a hole with my fingers, slowly so that snow slid to the outside rather than in. I looked up through it. Tiny stars swarmed the brighter ones and behind the smallest ones was the dust of fainter and farther stars, as if a rug had been beaten clean against the sky. Through the hole I could see nothing of the earth behind me. I floated off the shoulder of Orion, light years from solid ground. For hours I drifted.

I woke in the morning and dusted my way out of the bag. The world was just turning blue in the early light. My naked body flashed into the air for only a few seconds. Then I was wrapped in fleece and a variety of other petroleum products, my gloved fingers fumbling into plastic produce bags from a grocery store, grabbing nuts for breakfast. My frozen leather boots were determined not to conform to my feet. In a battle of cold wills, I stomped around in them. Finally I stopped and waited for both my feet and the boots to warm.

I looked across narrow sandstone walls a hundred feet high, constructed one after the next, each standing alone. They were the remnants of ancient, dissolved canyons. The labyrinth had fallen apart here, walls and passageways caved in, leaving odd towers standing around.

A strange sort of beauty, it is the last geological moment for this place, when canyons are worn into nothing but standing rocks. Early in the evolution of erosion, the layout is simple—chasm and rim, the first cut into the planet. That breaks down into complex feeder canyons, then inner slopes and dissected buttes much like the Grand Canyon. That carves into intricate shadow-box landscapes, and finally the land reaches its last breath—these spires and broken-down fins of rock—before completely opening itself. But even here, where there should be only wreckage, the objects are as sweet and piercing as broken porcelain, a kitchen floor scattered with the beautiful, dismembered remains of vases, tureens, cups, and decanters, their handles and rims hundreds of feet tall, stuck from the ground all around me.

I stood surveying the country with hands cupped together in a thin pair of gloves. Even the hectic routes of the Grand Canyon and the maze passages I had crawled through elsewhere in Utah seemed accessible compared to this. There was no true ground here, no place that I could claim as upper country or middle ground or low terrain. It was all slices and beds and huge pillars of rock barely remaining upright. Traveling through here we had found canyons driven by faults going nowhere and ending in blank walls. A route that seemed completely plausible looped back on itself, a surprising Möbius strip of ledges and nooks.

Low clouds stripped between the local landforms, tearing off in wet hunks. I noticed that Devin's sleeping bag was empty. Bootprints led away through snow. I heard a low moan from above. I looked up.

Behind camp stood a Cyclopean tower of sandstone. More than halfway up was a single cave of an eye socket, and Devin stood in it, a living pupil, feet firmly spread like a reckless desert god. He was catapulting a bullroarer over his head. Swung from a cord, it was a piece of Sonoran Desert ironwood he had carved so that its shape and weight spun fast into a scream. The faster he sent it in its orbit, the more fierce it sounded, like the vibrating low-to-high buzz of wind across a wire, like a shrieking animal. The cave was a parabola, a loudspeaker sending the increasing cry of the instrument out to the edges of reality.

The bullroarer spun down slowly until he caught the blade of wood in his right hand. Echoes continued. The land reverberated like a forged bell. I could see that this pleased him. He stood solidly, listening to the sound strike farther and farther faces, until it was finally inaudible.

I went back to my boots and my bag of nuts. A scrappy snowstorm moved through, whisking mares' tails of snow along bare rock. When Devin came down, he grabbed his own food from out of his pack and rounded over, squatting on the ground near me.

"Cold," he said.

I made an affirmative sound.

"Sleep much?" he asked.

"Too much. Or not enough. Hard to tell."

Snow rose with the wind, flirting over the ground. It gathered in creases in frozen soil and in pockets of rock. It collected on our clothes. Devin kept his eyes narrow in the wind.

"How far from here do you figure?" he asked.

"Maybe still an hour away. No more than that."

He made a sound of recognition, a grumble of vowels, studying the dry food in his own plastic bag, mixing it around before taking a handful, hoping to find some little taste treat, a nugget of chocolate.

I knew that the weather felt good to him. Cold, but good. The ground toyed with the storm, ripping the clouds into long streamers. This enhanced the shapes around us. The dampness and muffled light only increased the opulence of smell and color. Light changed constantly. It was a good morning.

His question about how far away was regarding a small clay pot of Anasazi origin. I had found it three years earlier while walking through here. At the time I was coming from another direction, through clusters of freestanding rock columns to the east, reaching an alcove on a snowy late-November day. I had found the earth in this place liberally broadcast with shattered pottery, stone tools, and a couple large pieces of painted bowls. The shape and exposure of the alcove, the slope of ground below it, they all were signals of occupation, a deserving place to be. I had come to my knees and brushed a light coating of sand from the pot's side, thinking it was only a smooth, dusty rock. I then touched it and heard its hollowness. It was the first complete pot I had ever found.

A clean, simple vessel, there was no paint on it at all. It was off-white, fired in a kiln within a reducing atmosphere so iron in the clay would not rust and turn the final product salmon. Its neck was as slender as that of a wine bottle. There were two loops for carrying, one of them broken leaving only nubs. It had been a water canteen. I took black-and-white photos of it and sketched it into my journal.

The presence of this pot stirred my fascination for the people once living in these interrupted canyons. Certainly, they had known the geographic significance of this place, how it was physically distinguished from surrounding terrain, from a sand and blackbrush plain to the north, scrollwork canyons to the south, and high cliffs far to the west and east. Each place no doubt had its own significance to these people, both in the capacity for hunting or traveling, and for how it penetrated the mind.

I did not have their lifelong experience, nor their cultural relevance of many generations in this landscape, but these shapes of rock were more or less the same now as they had been then. How similar, I wondered, was our recognition of them? Traveling in this country, I have often felt that within the human psyche is a perception that goes beyond personal heritage, that sees the land in the same crucial way across thousands of years. It is the part of us that is laid open here, an unaccountable sense of awe and apprehension in the face of a tumultuous landscape.

When I found this pot I had wished that I could communicate with these people, if for no other reason than to ask how they grasped this place around them. But they had long since migrated or died off, a far-flung desert culture dispossessed of identity by time. The pot was now the only information I had, round and resting on its side on the ground.

Devin had long been curious about this pot. It lay along the course of our travels, and I had told him I would take him there. He stood and closed his food bag, walking to his pack where he stuffed things away, his body announcing that it was time to go and find this pot. I moved to my pack and gathered things for the day.

Spires and narrow, unattached cliffs patrolled around us like enormous sentries. All of the ground was somewhere between six hundred feet up or seventy feet below, no base level anywhere. We came through joints in the rock, into sloping, cold clefts where we had to turn sideways inching our chests through, shoving our packs ahead, snow frantically commuting around us. The joints opened into lower basins and shelves.

I led Devin out a bridge of rock and at the other end stopped. I had been sure this was the way, but it tapered ahead of us, quickly becoming impassable. I turned, confused. This had been the way, hadn't it? Devin waited. I turned completely around twice.

"It was here," I said, not focusing on him. "Out along this run."

It was difficult to train my eyes on anything in particular, so many forms around us. "Or over there," I said, leaning my head forward as if that would help. I squinted. "Yeah, over there."

It is an easy place to become lost. It had happened to me here before, my first time in this region seven years before now, long before finding the pot. I had come to within a mile of here, the first thing I did after graduating from college, seventeen days into the desert. It was summer, June, a time of incredible heat. I had been traveling primarily by moonlight, but had gone out one morning planning to return to my shade camp before noon. I stretched myself as far into the heat as felt safe, but when I followed a route that I was certain would take me back to camp, I found myself shut out. Then, when I turned back, I only reached unfamiliar terrain, as if walls had grown while I was out. I tried other ways, scrambling into shallow, cloven passages, and was faced there with pour-offs that could not be climbed. Or some that were marginally possible, tempting me down, no way to get back up.

By early afternoon I had finished my water, pushing harder to find my way through, finding only frustration and turnarounds. Finally, I reached a high point looking straight down on my camp, gear left exactly as I had placed it at dawn. But no way to get to it. There were fissures that could not be jumped between here and there. I was near delirious in the heat, wanting to reach my hand out, touching the water in my camp less than three hundred feet away. I stood in the direct sunlight for maybe ten minutes. If I broke eye contact with the camp, throwing myself back down into this hurricane landscape, how would I find it again?

I did not reach camp until just before sunset, my body both electrified and languid, signs of chancy dehydration. I was at the time new to this sort of aimlessly articulated desert, and I crawled into the shade, clutching my water, trembling as if I had just scraped out from the grasp of a predator. I knew then how easily a person could vanish here. It is like walking through a constantly shifting illusion, routes appearing and decaying, the solvable and the utterly impossible snuggled so close to each other they cannot be told apart. I had thought then, *How can a person know a place like this?*

I walked with Devin behind me, showing him the way through a turning corkscrew, which came into a narrow wash of sand. This led to the overhang that held the pot. Pieces of broken ceramics lay all over the ground, and to my left as I entered was a portion of a painted bowl. I remembered it from before. I walked to an unmarked spot and dropped to my knees. Devin stood above me and watched.

My hand cupped into the stiffness of wet sand. Exactly where it should have been, precisely the shape that my hand remembered, was the curve of a pot. I sent my fingers beneath it and brought it out with a roll of my wrist. It came to the surface and cakes of sand fell free. In my hand was a white pot covered with black paintings. The paint was obviously old, nearly a thousand years, chipped and sanded faint in places. I immediately thought, *This isn't the same pot.*

Devin had studied my sketch of this artifact numerous times. He knew that it had not been decorated with paint, that I had written the words *Lino Gray* next to it on the sketch, identifying it as a plain style from a certain age. He had seen the photographs. Now he saw the pot and said over my shoulder, "It's painted."

"No," I said, swallowing. I scowled at it in confusion. No, it had not been painted.

I turned it slowly, like pushing a globe to see countries around the other side. More paintings came into view, triangles and lines. I felt a stillness around me, an undeniable sense of the impossible. I went back in my head, remembering when I first found this. I had stayed with the pot for two days. I had studied it for maybe ten hours in total, through different kinds of light and weather. There had been absolutely no paintings on it. *This cannot be,* I thought.

Low clouds entered from north of us, moving quickly as if going somewhere. They fell into corridors within the terrain. The corridors broke the clouds into rivers, long streamers that bucked and swirled through. The rock around us was rich with color, the hue of a red wine stain on a white tablecloth. Dampness reached my knees through my canvas pants. The pot remained in my hand. I don't know, maybe a minute or two. I looked up to Devin.

"I don't understand," I said.

"It's painted," he repeated.

"It wasn't, though. You saw the pictures. It wasn't painted at all."

He listened to me with only a remote part of his mind. He came down beside me and reached out delicately. I placed it in his hands.

It was the same pot. There was no question about that. But it was different. *Is this what happens out here,* I wondered? A person learns how to find the way through and the mantles keep opening, layers within layers, finally to those inconceivable?

"You suppose that the moisture from all this snow got into the clay?" he asked. "Last time you were here the ground must have been just enough drier."

I did not answer. He was right. Last time there was snow, but not enough to soak the alcove.

Holding it with one hand, Hamlet with a skull, he turned the pot in the same way I had, dipping his head to sneak around its bend. "So the melted snow saturates the soil and then moisture gets into the clay," he said. "It's porous material as it is. This somehow brings out the paintings. If it's dry, you can't see the paintings at all, and if it's wet you see everything. Right?"

I hesitated, then said, "Sure."

"So this is some kind of climatological phenomenon. A moisture thing."

"Sure," I said again.

This is how it works here, I thought. The slightest change alters the entire lay of the landscape, changing the ways of movement and exis-tence. Moisture decodes the map on a pot. The hallways of passages shift when I am not looking, like the drifting of Arctic sea ice. And yet nothing moves. The pot had been painted all along.

We passed the pot back and forth, set it down and looked around the area at other artifacts, then came back to it one at a time. I spent the rest of the morning considering the artwork, sitting in front of the vessel with my hands warm in my pockets, my back against a boulder. Snow dusted my shoulders.

Devin eventually went off to wander for the day, exploring other places, planning to meet me back at camp later. I stayed.

With the complicated lay of a map, black-on-white triangles and bands repeated themselves around the pot's body, holding my eyes. I could not easily accept this change. The pot had been clear in my mind for three years, and now black lines tapered gently over its curve. Some were horizontal, while others marked its slightly ovate equator. In places they had been worn faint, but in others the paint was still freshly dark. Paintings of this nature would never have been guessed had it been excavated or stolen. It would have sat dry in a display case or on an aluminum shelf in the catalog room of a museum, its art hidden.

Black-on-white styles like this were less commonly trade items among the Anasazi than were other styles such as red ware. This canteen was likely designed for local use, an artifact of the home. Rather than introducing it into far-reaching trade networks, sending it through barters of hybridized corn or sandals or obsidian knife blades from northern Arizona, it was manufactured for a particular chore, for one person carrying water during the dry seasons. It was for May and June. And for the cold of winter when springs and waterholes were frozen solid or scraped clean by wind.

I thought of someone charting a distance to be traveled, figuring on how much water would be needed, threading through this zone of complexity. People once knew the area that well. They chose this as a base, for reasons unknown settling and leaving goods here in these curves and rubble fields. What would the convolutions of this place have done to a human mind? Was it told in the designs on this pot?

Were the daily acts of people, their languages and ceramic wares, saturated and shaped by this landscape?

I see within pottery decoration from the Southwest—sharp geometric features, mostly acute or ninety-degree angles, curves, barbs, stair steps, and horizontal bands—the characteristic succession of this landscape: intricacy, parallelism, and interlocking patterns. My eye is stolen by the complexity of a Salado Polychrome, guided through the austere cataracts of a Kayenta black-on-white. At the same time I know that symmetry and rhythm are not monopolized by these artifacts. I have seen the same in a fractally carved Tlingit box from the Northwest coast of British Columbia, its bentwood inundated with eyes, ravens, hands, killer whales, and rows of polished cowrie shells; in the frescoed stone lid of a Mayan sarcophagus, as mirrored and contorted with detail as a rain forest; in the abacus designs of eastern Siberian embroidery. Everything speaks of the home landscape.

Newly appearing designs on an Anasazi pot

The work of the Southwest, the painting on this canteen, takes global themes and without sacrificing detail makes them crucially stark. It is a desert canyon motif: within harshness there is uniformity. There is a rule to this land, even here, and these people saw it. They learned to maneuver through it. They painted it on this vessel as if reminding themselves that all is not chaos.

I returned the pot to the ground in the late afternoon, thinking as I did that there are many ways to see this landscape, viewing it from a map or a plane, seeing it in the art of a pot, reading about it in a book, hearing or telling a story of it, and each has its own truth. But to be here, to witness its ceaseless metamorphosis, entire landforms and artifacts seeming to be rearranged, is inescapable. No matter where I walked from here, even if I closed my eyes, the land would continue to infuse me. This evanescent landscape is so coarse and knotted, so full of exposed potential, that there is not a single place where I could find refuge from it. I do not doubt that an Anasazi man or woman paused here and glanced around, wondering how things were now different, which route had become suddenly impassable, how the lay of the land had altered the mind. They must have known that they did not secure this land for themselves. It takes full possession of whomever passes through.

I walked slowly toward our camp and the Cyclops tower. At one point along the return path, at a high bench of solid rock, I stopped. Five miles away I saw a row of sandstone pillars standing out of a sea of canyons. I could not see where they began, or how far into the darkening canyons their trunks led.

One discovery opens another, and then another. Everything in this country is nested like Russian dolls. Even a solid artifact in front of me drew back into other levels. Schemes within schemes. Something as firm as a white, unpainted pot turned out to be something else.

I was disconcerted here. What makes the essence of this place so haunting is that it surpasses human imagination. Beneath the enriched lines of geology, this is not an easy land to bear.

I had believed that if I knew the very workings of the land and the people who had lived on it, I would be transformed. I would understand everything about this land and be able to see clearly through its eyes. But instead I stood here bemused. Today I found this changing pot, something that I thought could not be altered. If I cannot trust the indivisible, what can I trust? I remained standing in the damp wind and the coming night, holding onto the ground with my eyes and my thoughts, afraid to let go.

ISLAND

Sea of Cortés

I tried to keep my eyes open. They burned with salt. Seawater and saliva drooled down my chin. I just let it run. Another wave came, exploding over the bow, striking my body. It seemed as if the boat might fly, but its weight brought it down, driving it again into the water. I took my hand from the gunwale for only an instant and swiftly rubbed out my eyes beneath smudged sunglasses, looking ahead to La Isla, the island. It sat eight miles away still, a collection of rocky desert peaks closely guarding one another against the sea. Waves had beaten its flanks into cliffs. Not a single person lives there. There is no water. Another wave took me like a backhanded smack and I lost my vision.

I had come far south from Utah, across Arizona and into the

northwestern reaches of Mexico. This is where the world disintegrates. Chunks of formless rock as big as the Dead Sea are left scattered across this Sonoran Desert, connected by veins of eroded volcanoes. The seams and hinges and sweet domes that dignify southern Utah are lost here, reduced to serrated rubble. Everything that remains in this part of the desert, stabbing up from huge basins hundreds of miles long, is all that is left, eroded and upthrust cores of a land that once stood. A few pieces of the continent remain just above the surface of the sea this far south, islands shaped like chewed bones, remnants of the former earth.

Beside me sat a woman named Alyssa Van Schmus, a river and rescue ranger on vacation from Canyonlands National Park in Utah. Directly beside her sat Regan Choi, leaning into the waves so that they broke evenly across her shoulders, lifting as they passed so that the water poured down her back, a kind of motion birds use when scooping water into their beaks. She was soaked, spitting and clearing her eyes. Behind her stood Devin Vaughan holding onto a vertical metal post fused to the hull. We looked like lumps of clay, snapped into life only when waves hit us. Behind all of us stood Antonio Salsueta running with his left hand a 115-horsepower outboard motor that propelled this twenty-five-foot fishing *ponga*—a slender, high-walled skiff with a flared bow—to the crests of waves, then down their backsides. He wore bright yellow waders held up by suspenders, and a matching yellow slicker.

Devin and I had known Antonio for a few years. He was one of the most accomplished ponga fishermen out of the nearest mainland Mexican town. He was the man we could absolutely trust to get us out to the island through the hard winds of February—*el tiempo loco,* he called it.

He used wonderful economy with the waves, slicing through them, utilizing an impact on one side of the boat to throw us into better position, grabbing a long line of high, frothy crests while leaving the propeller to scream in the air. The hull of the ponga smashed down over and over like concrete striking concrete in hard, shuddering blows. I saw sunlight beneath my feet, quick flashes through thinning fiberglass.

Antonio was hauling us out with two weeks of supplies—mostly fresh water—to La Isla, which is not the island's true name, but will do for now. It is one of numerous rocks sticking up from the Sea of Cortés, also known as the Gulf of California. We had been leapfrogging the islands to reach La Isla, waiting for the winds to die just enough as we made one crossing and then the next. Last night the five of us slept in the cove of an island north of here, cooking chiles and tortillas in the wind shelter of sea scrub. Now we were making the final passage.

Antonio cut the throttle midway from the previous island to La Isla. His left arm, used to steer, was tiring. For the short break we rose to wave tops, able to see around like children on tiptoes, then sank into troughs where we saw nothing but water and white stars of foam casting overhead. As we lifted again I got my closest view of La Isla. It was crowded with crests and summits, and incredibly steep crevices lined between. Its edges offered no obvious landing. Antonio knew of the place, though, a wash meeting the sea on the east side where we would land and the four of us would leave him, hauling our supplies toward the island's interior.

The island is little more than a few miles long, made of mountains nearly two thousand feet tall, rocky spines lifting directly out of the sea. Even with no fresh water on the island, somehow people once lived there. They were a tribe of wild people. The local Seri culture—a fierce people in themselves who were once hunted for sport by the Spanish at three pesos a head—has stories of giants living on this island. These giants spoke by singing or crying, and could outfish, outfight, outswim, and outlive anyone. They were notorious gamblers who easily bet their lives, and just as easily lost, dying without hesitation. It was said that they could kill a sea lion by throwing a single rock from shore. They were, according to the Seri, the only people who could survive on this barren rock.

I remembered a story that seemed now to have been about this island. When I was much younger, a chapter from a children's book, *The Phantom Tollbooth*, was read to me in bed each night. I was captured by a tale that went this way:

> Once upon a time, this land was a barren and frightening wilderness whose high rocky mountains sheltered the evil winds and whose barren valleys offered hospitality to no man. Few things grew, and those that did were bent and twisted and their fruit was as bitter as wormwood. What wasn't waste was desert, and what wasn't desert was rock, and the demons of darkness made their homes in the hills. Evil creatures roamed at will through the countryside and down to the sea.

For whatever reason, in my child's mind, the place had sounded comforting. The evil creatures were not busy terrifying anyone. They simply roamed at will. I enjoyed the notion of grotesque things wandering quietly with calm expressions upon their ugly faces. There would be rocky caves in which to hide, uncommon truths to be revealed in long night conversations with demons—*to talk with demons, now there's something!* A person would have to be cunning to get around. Water would need to be found, and places to sleep. I was inspired.

Of course, a young prince came to this place in the name of goodness and truth. I hated the prince. I was shocked, but somehow not surprised, to hear that he charged against the rough country with troops, and then brought settlers from far away. Each day the wilderness was "attacked anew" until the Kingdom of Wisdom was established. Buried in covers I listened to this tale of horror, sinking lower so that only my eyes showed, wondering what happened to all of these intriguing things, the frightening wilderness and barren valleys. They now harbored the emotionless bustle of cities, people haggling in the markets, and rulers who waged wars on each other to solve their hateful divisions. But where did they go, the demons of darkness? Where would I have to go to find them?

The island ahead was the place. Its cliff-lined arroyos are overrun with impenetrable cactus forests. Most of the ground is nearing vertical, continually calving off. Whatever flat ground there is has a blanket of agaves with poison needle-tips. The wind is ceaseless. This is what I had heard of this place.

"*Veinte minutos,*" Antonio shouted, tugging on the engine's cord. Twenty minutes. He cranked the engine and we surged up the side of a wave, as if coming up the roof of a circus tent.

Within a day of landing we had an inland base camp established, our gear and water hauled up one of the arroyos. Most of our attention focused on the island's interior, but on occasion we found routes to the rare and barely sheltered beaches.

On our eighth day on the island I walked a beach alone, having found my way down from the ridges, one step at a time for an hour as I negotiated the fragile holds, every object loose and crumbling in hand. Here I found a fishing encampment in a bare hollow in one of the headlands, just out of the waves. There was no sand anywhere, only black boulders fallen into the water from overhead cliffs.

This camp seemed like a haphazard garrison. Pieces of wind-shredded fabric were tied to unraveling nylon ropes, both bleached by the sun. A sheltering overhead *ramada* made of stripped agave leaves and a low rock wall crouched against the cliff, taking advantage of sort of a natural overhang. Small rock shelters lay scattered about, horseshoe-shaped, only large enough for a grown man to curl into, escaping the full force of the wind. I walked from shelter to shelter, crouching in each and finding the remains of men's lives.

This is the farthest reach for fishermen driven west by the dwindling fish yields along the coast. It is the last place they want to go, where they sometimes find themselves stranded in the heedless wind. The word among fishermen is that the island is eerily comfortless, more so than a person would expect, and one Mexican man admitted that every time he sleeps here he has nightmares. There is a common story of a light seen on its shore and of ponga fishermen arriving late, crashing through the waves in anticipation of joining another stuck party. Upon landing they find no light and no other fishermen, a sense of sudden loneliness that makes this island seem thoroughly uninhabitable.

On occasion, a few of these people will perish, running out of water and trying the sea as an escape, their pongas overturning in storm waves on clear and windy days. At least this is a more fitting, proper death among fishermen. To die stranded on this island is a condemnation, an unimaginable horror.

In one of the wind shelters, held safe beneath a rock, were hand-drawn dominoes cut from a piece of cardboard and laminated with clear tape. It was a game for waiting out the days, huddled in the rocks, and I envisioned the man playing long after his interest in the game had faded, anything to keep his mind away from the wind.

Within another shelter was a white, nearly crystalline rock that had been broken to small, workable pieces. The assemblage had been neatly arranged, and a number of pieces were chosen for their sturdiness, fashioned then into hand tools. A knife. A scraper. A small hand drill. I wondered if the maker had been merely preserving the sharpness of his own metal tools by using these, or if he was inventing a distraction to keep his eyes off of the whitecapped sea. I picked up each tool, turned it in my hand, and set it back where I had found it.

I was a scavenger here, studying the prints of people as soon as they were gone, coming to pick through their wind-blasted leavings. I lifted their discarded fishing equipment, pitted floaters and monofilament, and an abandoned bag of salt, trying to discover what is indelible about my species, what is left behind that tells of our passage into this land.

Beyond the camp, closer to the water, I found the mummified body of a young sea lion, skin pulled into tight parchment around its skull, flippers as stiff as tire rubber. It smelled less of death and more of the sea, keeping with it memories of the water. The beach was strewn with such vestiges. Only the hard parts of living things remained: the hollow, geometric forms of abandoned urchins, the vertebral disk of a whale, and an infinity of shells eroded to their most lasting shapes of spirals and arches. I picked up one of the strutlike wingbones of a pelican, running my finger along its rasp of knobs. Things come to this island to be reduced, I thought. The jagged peaks stand like a collection net, grabbing every crumb and bit before it is worn to nothing, the shells and wings and the endmost longings of Mexican fishermen.

Even the island's interior is rapidly coming apart, wearing down to its core. Everything is surfaced by pieces of broken rock. The large boulders are ruined, making climbing through the ridges perilous, nothing solid underfoot, each handhold flaking away with any misdirected weight. La Isla is in a state of remarkable, unstoppable erosion. Only the strangest pieces of the land remain, malformed jabs and great belfries of rock. There is not a single curve to the place. The rocks are of the sort that you would never want near your house, notched and crude, easily drawing blood.

In eight days of walking I had found no sign that the fishermen had come away from the beaches into the interior of the island. I did not find habitual foot trails or cans left from lunch. There was far better shelter away from the sea cliffs, rents that cut back from the wind and boulder floors well below the ridge tops, yet fishermen went only far enough to gather firewood from dead ironwood trees or to cut apart an agave heart with a machete for roasting at camp. It is as if this island offered them nothing but a thin perimeter of land safe from the sea, a place to secure their fiberglass pongas. The interior is uninviting.

Yet at the same time I had found sites of indigenous pottery and numerous middens where those called giants by the Seri had hauled shellfish from the sea cliffs into the island's crags and minarets. These original inhabitants seemed to have operated on an entirely different assumption than the fishermen, living inside rather than loitering along the edges. I had come across their remains in the most unlikely spots, shells gathered on a barbarous ridge, difficult to access from any side, and bits of pottery just below a friable summit. This left me with the sense that they had not been indiscreet brutes, as they were sometimes portrayed by the Seri. They did not spend their lives huddling along the shore where there was ample food, clinging hand to mouth to their survival. Something else had captured their attention, something inside the island.

I walked back through the ponga fishermen's beach camp, stopping where a nylon rope had been mindfully hand-braided, and then was cast aside unfinished, as if the wind had slowed and the man saw a narrow window of escape. The making of a rope had become a suddenly trivial venture. I gathered from what I saw around me that the fishermen used this island as only the most desperate measure: a place where they longed for their wives and children, for tortillas cooked on huge metal disks in the yard, eaten just as they come off, the air bladders of fish thrown on the skillet and consumed like chips, nights of drunken singing in the familiar vigor of town streets, repayment for time spent on this horrible island.

The giants had lived differently here. By virtue of numerous generations, they must have realized the potential in every facet of this island, arroyos good for cactus fruits in certain years, rock outcrops of stone useful in shaving open the hearts of agaves (a plant like a three-foot-tall artichoke with knife blades for leaves), or the scoured basins I came across on the island's southwestern side where water would gather in even the lightest rain. Beyond this purely functional landscape, though, I imagine that they found intimate quiescence among the many interior escarpments, places of rest and composure, a most basic need of even the most rustic people.

While walking the scattering ridges high above here, I envisioned small numbers of people on this island, customary for isolated hunting and gathering groups. I saw them moving in fours or fives, perhaps alone, to fetch whatever was needed from the island confines, recognizing around them the serenity of this homescape, a known and enclosed territory. To an unfamiliar, outsider's eye there might only be struggle and ferocity in this topography, but the evidence of archaeology leads to a reliance on the island's insides, a place where people lived for unknown centuries, likely millennia.

I knew what the fishermen knew about this place, and also had an inkling of what the giants might have known. The inside of this island is touched with what is both unfathomable and enchanting at once, capes of peaks worn to falling, and the potent seclusion of inner canyons. I passed through rusting artifacts from the fishermen and then up a cliff-walled arroyo, leaving the beach. As I walked, skirting between the arms and trunks of thirty-foot-tall cardón cacti, along blades of canyon floors, the sound of the sea left me. I slipped into the island.

I once spoke with an archaeologist, a man named Thomas Bowen, who conducted research on La Isla over a seven-year period, reflecting as he went on aspects of botany and oral history and the influence of sea currents, whatever seemed pertinent to understanding its former inhabitants. Bowen and his small team exercised rare and heartening concern in their work, the sort one would use in handling fragile family documents, strongly debating whether they should even dig a small hand trench to sample charcoal from these people. The island, it seemed to him, was in perfect condition, an incredible display of unchecked landforms and human remains that needed no modern disturbance.

He loaded his pack, carrying research and survival supplies across the interior, finding quickly that it is much more inaccessible than one might imagine, especially for so small a space, no more than sixteen square miles. He covered as much land as was possible over those seven years, but still, the majority of his map was left unmarked, places that he was never able to reach. At the boundaries of these unexplored regions he found twelve habitation caves littered with butchered animal bones, pieces of pottery, and other small artifacts, and then fifty-three hand-built stone circles out in the open, ample evidence that people had established themselves here.

He once wrote, "It is not merely that there are a few undamaged sites, but rather that the archaeological record of the entire island is essentially intact. In some cases, sites looked to us as if their occupants had stepped out only minutes before our arrival. . . ."

He complained to me that modern science has little room for an island like this. There is too much pressure from the scientific community to arrive and rapidly possess the needed information, then abandon the place in a quick attempt to have work reviewed and published. The island itself, he said, requires slow and sincere observation on many levels. Most people who come to this island in their swiftness are left with the impression that it is too severe for any long-term human presence. "My first impression there was bafflement," he said. "Never had I seen topography like this. And then people living within it. I came away from my first time shaking my head, not sure of how to understand this place."

Of the fifteen or so researchers that he knew working at different times on La Isla, only two ever came upon these rich archaeological remains. Some claimed the island as utterly pristine, impossible for human survival, a perfect scientific petri dish. It was as if they did not want this place marred by the inelegant remains of humans, and were in the same breath unwilling to spend time behind the stern outer walls, in the realms where people once lived.

When Bowen spoke of his work on La Isla, it was as if describing a long-ago vision, his words slowing and becoming saturated with memory. "I have to confess that part of my interest in going was not scientific," he said. "I don't want to make too much of this, but I found the island to be a very spooky place. In a luring way. The same for those who were with me. There must be some aspect to the topography, the vegetation, the geology, I don't know. It somehow gives you cues. I could never put my finger on it. There is something on this island that comes subconsciously, telling you that this place is unlike any other."

Walking up from the beach, I climbed into a steep plunge of rock facades. Some of the spaces within were heavily shadowed and I rested there. I sat in a crotch where boulders had fallen together, adjusting my body until I found an acceptable position, one where a fist of rock was not centered on my spine or pressing against my shoulder blade. I settled on my muscles.

The island was a shroud around me, crag-faced walls lifting over a thousand feet behind my back, leading to a series of peaks, each a different shape and height. I scanned the vertical distances, both looking for a way up and filling myself with this sensation of hugeness and fragility. It was like looking into a fire, watching the flames spread and shift, no sense of loss or gain, only movement.

Viewing this island from a ponga or from along a beach, it seems like a place that can be created in the mind. It is open territory, undefined, full of truth or terror or grace depending on how the story is told. The researchers who did not want to contend with humanity, who wanted a place beyond our familiar reach, saw an island that had never been lived upon. But instead, sitting in the shade of these chapped boulders,

I could see what Bowen had discovered, that this landscape was already made. With its staggering and fragmented topography it was nothing that I could re-form in my mind, not a story or a concept of entertainment or personal satisfaction. It was alive and flashing over my head, leaving me with an enduring sense of what is primitive.

This place is what is truly meant as primitive, not something that is clumsily barbaric or unable to reveal profundity on its surface. It is deeply visceral, holding the darker side of human longing, and at the same time able to convey sentience, a knowledge of life. There should be a name for it, I thought, a reference that I could easily use. Essence or breath of life. It is perhaps known as *barakah,* an Arabic word for the power within, something that can be carried in a vessel of water, in a person, in a stone, that can be surrendered and passed on but is indestructible. This is why I come. It is here in the crumbling remains of La Isla.

Wherever we walked we were followed by ravens. There were two of them, one easily recognized by a feather missing from its left wing. Both were rough looking, their wings tattered by the wind and by hard landings in cactus and on rocks. Curious about our presence, the ravens marked us mile by mile as we roamed through the island's insides, into abandoned castles of mountains and along the floors of arroyos. Sometimes they followed closely, perching on one cactus and then the next, all the time testing us with different calls and voices—coarse shouts, sighs, and low tones like a marimba rattled by felt mallets. The calls seemed directed toward us, or at least were about us.

They repeated each call a few times, then switched to a new sound as if trying to find a language we might understand.

Walking along, I saw one of these ravens in an ironwood tree in the floor of an arroyo, knitting furiously with its beak. It had prey, pulling away strands of blood and meat. The appearance of blood, of moist innards, was scandalous. *Water,* I thought. I came close enough that the bird startled, dropping its meal. I walked up to the remains and knelt.

It was a spiny-tailed iguana pulled inside out like a T-shirt. This, I realized, is how the birds get their beaks through the roughage of skin down to the sweet meat, explaining the many inside-out and disrobed iguanas and chuckwallas we had been seeing. *This is what survival is here,* I thought, picking up the grisly carcass, its blood-smear drying quickly in the air. *Tearing the insides out of things, getting under the skin.*

The island is a refuge of reptiles. Huge chuckwallas and spiny-tailed iguanas slide in and out of rocks, dinosaur movements that I caught every few minutes from the corner of my eye. They are guardians, ancient creatures with unexcitable expressions on their bony faces; long, scratching claws, and backs encrusted with beads and sharp scales. The ravens seemed humorous and flexible, as curious as the four of us as they skated through the sky, while the lizards—their eyes unaccommodating—ruled the earth below. Generations of dead bodies were practically everywhere, along each arroyo, up in the pinnacles, and lying among sea gull feathers on the beach.

By far, these lizards were the largest creatures here. When we walked, we found no sign of coyotes or rabbits on the island, and no bighorn sheep. Absent were also creosote, ocotillo, and brittlebush, each a common plant on the mainland of the Sonoran coast, and even some of the nearby islands. No cactus wrens built nests in the crooks of cholla cacti here and no curved-bill thrashers hunted around with their ruby eyes. Quail did not race from shrub to shrub. It was as if the island had once been burned out, leaving a smoking hulk on which only certain beasts could live. It was a place too harsh for common creatures.

There were no animal trails. This was something I noticed early. I had never walked where there were no animals even as large as a rabbit, and on this island whenever I stepped into a place that seemed easy, I expected a clearing and a shaving off of thorns and barbs from the nearest branches. There was no such thing. The island belonged only to lizards, cacti, catclaws, elephant trees, palo verde, and iron-wood trees, and a pair of ravens. I walked around absorbing the sensation, this idea that I was teetering at the edge of the earth, a place avoided by most living creatures. It was here that I could feel the breath of life as if it were roaring through the air, the land completely raw beneath it.

We carried with us a hand-drawn map that we added to with pencil as we went along. In the morning Alyssa scanned the open map, her gear still on her back. She crouched over the map like a crab, her long, flexible legs bending at the knees so that her body swayed as she examined one corner of the island and the next. She used a compass to match bearings. Devin leaned over her shoulder and marked a new arroyo that we had seen.

Alyssa is tall, late twenties, her hair short and sandy blonde. Her muscles are slender, bounding with high-strung and observant energy. In Utah, working for the National Park Service, she sometimes wears a bulletproof life vest and carries an M-16 rifle in a waterproof container. On the job she hangs a stunning amount of climbing gear and rescue rope from her body. Out here she travels with a light pack and little clothing, her skin darkening under the sun. She can sleep on the ground amazingly well, curling into a petite animal ball in the middle of the day, covering herself from the wind with a single sheet of fabric until she is hardly visible. She was a good creature for this island.

When we decided where we were on the map, it was folded away and the four of us moved west, fanning across a broad arroyo. Mountains stood around us as we traveled. The object of the day was to reach the island's far side. Crossing the five or so miles was slow as we picked between drainages and plains of cactus forests. We took few breaks, marching up a great slope of boulders, arroyos working back into sheer walls in all directions.

In the late afternoon we reached the western brink. This entire side is a slew of cliffs and boulder-clogged chutes. We stopped above an eight-hundred-foot palisade. As we rested there we found pottery. First a small piece, then five larger ones, then twenty. Soon we found the remains of almost entire pots, piecing them together like puzzles. Much of the ceramics were of the "eggshell" variety, some of the thinnest, most finely manufactured pottery in all of the Americas. Huge five- and ten-gallon ollas would have safeguarded these people's fresh water, the pot walls as thin and engineered as a wine glass.

Because of this thinness, the ratio of a vessel's capacity to its weight is less than half of those constructed by the Mogollon, the Hohokam, and the Anasazi.

No one is certain who made this pottery. What little ceramics were created by the Seri in the past hundred years—a skill that has all but died out—are generally thick and roughly finished, and tempered by animal dung leaving pores through which water can evaporate. This ancient "eggshell" pottery is finely finished, sometimes no thicker than three millimeters, and made almost without pores, allowing water to remain protected within. Some who study prehistoric ceramics claim it as some of the finest in the world.

While we milled around, exploring this surprising volume and quality of pottery smashed on the ground, Alyssa found a small clay figurine. It immediately drew the rest of us. From my conversation with Thomas Bowen, I knew that this island had never produced a single figurine.

The object was broken in half and the second piece could not be found. We gathered around this fawn-colored fetish, passing it from hand to hand. It was no bigger than a soup spoon. It was a curved shell of clay tapering toward a long point, the same style as fetishes I had seen from the mainland desert. Lines had been etched into it prior to firing: belts, rows, and offset chevrons. Complete, it would have been a tall, slender figure, likely ending at the bottom in a single extension of clay as narrow as a stiletto heel. The upper end—the piece Alyssa had found—was a humanlike torso broadly unfolding to horizontal shoulders. I knew from other intact figurines I had seen that the head, broken off here, would have risen from the body like a stylized dagger.

Here was an object that was human, but at the same time stretched and distorted, a graceful but misshapenly numinous person. I remembered that the owners of these fetishes were said to have fasted in caves. On the fourth night spirits emerged from the cave walls, each spirit the same shape as a clay figurine, ghostly and tapered bodies riddled with pulsing, zigzag imagery. Some of these would enter the body of the waiting person. I rotated the clay-brown fetish thinking about this ethereal image. I passed it to Alyssa, who cradled it in both hands, as if it were a beloved memento long-lost.

These kinds of objects likely had many uses over thousands of years, some spiritual, some not. Many modern Seri claim that if their ancestors used them at all, they were children's playthings. At the same time the Seri gave a name to the fetishes that basically translates to "things that the singing giants gave life to." The older Seri, who recall stories of the giants, have said that shamanic powers were used to animate these objects. To do what, no one remembers.

Another possible function revealed by Seri stories is that the figurines were buried in times of trouble or buried with the dead, or that they are associated with childbirth and the highly structured traditions that the Seri hold over such events. These are all likely true as the objects were passed from generation to generation, from one culture to the next even, the use changing according to the era. Eventually, into historic times, the use of pottery dwindled in this part of Mexico and the kiln-firing of clay figurines was abandoned.

I once had a conversation with archaeologist Richard White, who had studied at least ten thousand clay figurines resembling the one we encountered on La Isla. At the time he was excited about a recent discovery of numerous similar clay figurines near Tucson, Arizona, dating back to 300 B.C., many bearing the same markings of bands and offset chevrons as those from this area. After having found nothing else worldwide that looked anything like these Seri-style figurines, the finds in Arizona produced a sudden connection three hundred miles across the desert. Then, as if an afterthought, he mentioned to me a single clay figurine that had come out of Siberia.

"Of course there's really nothing that I can do with this information with only one artifact to show for it," he said. "But this Siberian figurine is a dead ringer for the ones I've seen from the area you're talking about in Mexico. I've looked at a lot of material from around the world and found nothing else like these Seri figurines. I believe there is something to it, that in Mexico we're looking at the vestiges of some extremely old traditions."

Whatever their lineage was, this was the most lasting thing that these people left behind, a solid part of their lives that had survived the intense weathering of this island. When it came back to me, I turned the fetish over and over. It told me only one thing, that people here had carried something with them, something distinctly human that could not be used for common physical tasks such as fire-starting or prying open the shell of an oyster. It had another purpose, one that was now much like the atmosphere of the island, unknowable and filled with poignancy.

I handed it off to Devin, who held it up so that it was outlined by the sky. "The work of barbarians," he said. "Like us." He brought it down and passed a finger over the etchings.

Devin passed it on to Regan, who gathered herself into painting position, setting a coarse sheet of watercolor paper on her knees, backing against a boulder with the broken item in her hand. She did not busy herself with undue marvel, or hold it in the air gasping at its potential. She set brush to paper, a few drops of water in her paint cup, and began her record of this curious object.

I walked through a narrow, steep arroyo late in our travels on La Isla, moving alone from our base camp to explore the afternoon desert. The others were doing the same, exploring alone. Crumbling cords of volcanic rock took me into the bowels of a mountain. Whenever there was a good clearing, groves of giant cardón cacti appeared, similar in stature to saguaros but much larger with twenty or thirty arms and

Pitahaya agria cactus common on the island; genus Stenocereus massive, obese trunks. They surrounded each other, interlocked pillars forty feet tall. Their interior sanctuaries were shaded and cool. I ducked through them as if I were a child slipping between the legs of adults standing in important conversation.

As I walked I came upon a sea of bayonet-leafed agaves, then turned back only to be stopped by wall-to-wall toils of pitahaya agria cacti eight feet tall, too densely grown and spined to allow even my hand through. The cacti looked busied and alive, hundreds of probing arms ducking in and out of each other. I peered into the thicket and could see only darkness in the center. I turned around to find another way. I went into backtracks and climbs, scrambling through worn and disintegrating boulders into steep-walled pits. Finally I walked up from the arroyo across an open moonscape of wind-carved rocks. When I reached a pass, the magnificent blue stage of the sea opened beyond and far below. Other islands sprawled in the distance, slender and barren, like dead iguanas and chuckwallas themselves, skin dried back, bones poking through with ugly grins, and sharp teeth. Arroyos dropped steeply beneath my feet toward the foaming margin of waves. The sea worked hard against the island.

I went along a scaffolding of ridges with the moon hanging in front of me; it was a daytime gibbous over one of the nearby islands. I stopped and viewed the shapes before me. Each thing I could see visually settled into the other, fixing an asymmetrical alignment. I saw in that moment a relationship, something that I had so far been unable to find in this chaotic terrain. It was an alliance between the next island out, the uninhabited coast of Baja, the sea, the moon pale and as dusty as a moth's wing, and the island ridges broken in front of me. Like passing through the alignment of the snake in the rock fins of Utah, there was a hugeness to the spheres I saw here. Everything seemed held in place, bound together as if by a single, endless thread, every action and object hinged one to the next. I thought that this may have once seemed commonplace for the people who lived here, this feeling that rock, moon, time, and breath are the same stark entity.

I looked down, and in the swaybacked saddle ahead of me saw a constellation of white shapes. They were shells on the ground, a thousand feet above the water. When I reached the saddle, I squatted and thumbed through the mound, digging scallops and periwinkles from the hard desert surface. These were the result of decades of meals, people hauling shellfish from the sea to eat them here. Why so far up? It was as if they had grabbed what they needed for food and retreated into the rough protection of the island. So little is known about these people that to imagine them one way or another is truly unfair. I went by what I saw in front of me, a collection of shells carried all the way from the sea.

I turned one of the shells in my hand, picturing the other hands before me, methodical motions, bony, strong fingers lifting out flesh and putting it in the mouth. They had done this in view of the same moon, the same other islands. I considered the fact that they may not have known anything about the linear time of watches and calendars. For the people of this island the cycles of the sky repeated themselves without end. Changeless generations of families stretched forward and back beyond horizons of time. Infinity would have been at the tip of the tongue, no beginning and no end anywhere in sight. The person who last held this shell, I thought, was of an eternal mind.

Over the days we had found other scant remains of shell middens, some worked points of stone, a few pieces of thin mustard-colored pottery, the broken figurine, and the bones of a sea turtle in a high inland cave. The turtle bones had ignited our knowledge of the people who once lived here, telling us that they had captured something of the sea, a huge and heavy creature, then hauled it all the way into the desert over picket fences of cliffs and ridgelines. Had it been eaten? Had the carapace been wildly painted as was common in Seri ritual? Had the settled serum of turtle blood been used as a salty substitute for water, another custom of the Seri?

The story told by the Seri is that in the end the people of this island became plants and rocks. Two prominent peaks on the island, Hast Cmaam and Hast Ctam, visible from some distance, are respectively male and female, specific entities standing side by side. The people not only became part of the landscape; they turned directly into the land-scape itself, losing their flesh and converting into everything around.

Another story is that the Mexican army came to get these giants. La Isla's residents had been isolated from European contact possibly until the 1800s, maybe even until the final decades of that century. In the scorching summer of 1890 the Mexican gunboat *Demócrata* arrived and loaded a hundred or so people onto its deck from the island. Whatever happened next is missing from the ship's logbook. It is known that two years later the *Demócrata* hauled two hundred members of the Yaqui tribe out to sea and shoved them off, leaving none alive, so the fate of La Isla's inhabitants can be imagined.

This story does not at all conflict with what the Seri say, as stories tend to tell only what is most pertinent to the observer. However it happened, the giants of La Isla, indeed, turned to stone, their only remnants being these cliffs and ridges and the hand tools they left behind.

Perhaps the historic Seri called them giants as a form of ancestor worship, much like the way we look back at the Egyptians in the late centuries b.c., people larger than life. The people of La Isla were some of the final vestiges of an influential and ancient culture that dwindled and was eventually finished off by the Mexican army. Or perhaps the idea of giants was inspired by well-traveled people, maybe those with impressive boats thousands of years ago who were able to easily stride great distances across the earth or sea; it is said that they could walk across the water from Baja to the mainland, using the islands like stepping stones. Whatever it is, I imagine that the Seri term *giant* does not match the Europeans' simple Jack and the Beanstalk figure. Instead it refers to something older, a hugeness within the mind, people who perhaps were able to live in a place of no water, beyond the means of ordinary humans.

With shells in my hand I looked back up to the moon, the far island, and the Baja coast, taking this knowledge of shells gathered by people, adding it to the view. Whoever the giants were, whatever finally happened to them, these shells were theirs. This island was their home. I scanned the setting around me, a landscape of giants, and the island under my feet seemed to creak open, cliffs dropping in every direction.

In this moment I no longer formed the landscape in my mind. The landscape formed me. I did not choose from which angle I saw it and

I did not decide how an experience in it should be interpreted. The angles became so acute that there was no choice about which way to view them. I bent with the land until my mind matched the profiles that I saw.

When we speak of transformation, this island is where our words finally take us. Crouched at the brink of this ridge, I was taken by the land. I let the shells fall through my fingers as I looked across the ridge, watching the moon hover above the sea. The lines connecting the moon, the island, and these shells ran straight through me. I was a member of this eternity. I thought I might stop breathing. I had to concentrate to hold myself here. I filled my lungs and exhaled. I moved my body, the flex of muscles and rustle of clothing keeping me within my mind. It is so easy, I thought. So easy to be carried away. Isn't this what I wanted, though, to be turned to stone? I smiled ironically at myself.

True. But not yet.

I stood, my body responding to my command. I turned slowly, examining the whole of my view. A Seri deity called Land Maker, *Hant Caai,* is the one who made this torturous landscape. I remembered this and the memory held me in place, giving me an idea of future and past. Everything here was once flat; that was the past. It would be flat again, eroded out of sight, and that was the future. *Hant Caai* once broke into the smooth, former earth to bring up a more tempting and protective landscape, the one I saw today. He exposed these terrible jags and pits. He did this land-making by singing. I wondered about his song, the one that I heard during each of these rare moments in my life.

As I stood at the shell midden thinking of the creation of this jagged landscape, a honeybee appeared and hovered before my face. Its shrill, industrious buzz was as waking as a copper bell struck by a hammer. It questioned me. Did I have pollen? Was there sweetness in my eyes? Perhaps it had come on a wind, sent here from Baja, off course from the hive. Soon it would be a husk in a wash, silent among rocks in this island of diminution. I would not yet surrender my pollen. The bee shrieked away, leaving me only with the sound of wind, Land Maker's irresistible song.

CRAGS

Southwest Arizona

I held a slingshot, the firing stone drawn to my eye. A bony desert jackrabbit was my target, its long ears as transparent as vellum, a pink filigree of veins showing through. I saw vulnerability in these veins. A lanky, swift animal, it still had the fragility of life and that is where I focused. The desert spread around it, around both of us, as perilous and unapproachable as the surface of hell.

I lifted one foot off the ground to come closer, keeping my aim firm in case the rabbit should bolt. This stone I used, a volcanic pebble of southwest Arizona, was not round. There is nothing round in this country. It would have four or five feet of truth when fired, then it would lean well away from its mark.

I had been following this jackrabbit for three hours, watching it burst, tracking it for half a mile on this warm February day, sliding up close only to see it fly again. Four days away from a food cache, I was hungry. All that remained until this next supply was rice, raisins, powdered milk, and several dehydrated marbles of homemade *posole*. I had already eaten the fruits of the fishhook cactus and the red flowers of the *chuparosa,* which tasted sweet like cucumbers. I had eaten the tangy leaves of the sow plant and a portion of a rare and brilliant fruit belonging to the night-blooming cereus cactus. I would certainly not perish from hunger between here and the cache. I only craved this taste, rabbit cooked over a fire.

An alertness suddenly came to its eyes. The rock fired from my slingshot. A high-pitched whine stung the air, ending in a bullet of dust just to the side of my target. The rabbit's compact body uncoiled like a striking snake and it left. I lowered the slingshot, watching a graceful line of anxiety carry the rabbit away from me. It sailed across the ground, in and out of washes, between creosote bushes, over a rise.

I had followed it far enough. The slingshot hung loosely from my left hand. I abandoned my sense of disappointment. I looked around. My partner, Irvin Fernandez, was out here hunting also. I scanned for his shape but could not find him, looking across Easter Island heads of rock, massive, solid cores of volcanoes. Among them, down between their shadows, ran plains of broken stones, each a size that could fit easily in the hand. That he was there at all was a strange sensation, another human in these endless, desolate miles.

Everything around me was a predatory landscape. From northwest

Mexico into southwest Arizona the mountains are opened blocks, the throats of volcanoes shoved up through laminations of hardened magma, extinct caldera walls, and dikes grotesquely stretched out like melted glass. The landmark mountains are nothing but fine pinnacles, the only things left standing at the far edge of erosion.

Unlike La Isla with its exfoliating exterior, here all that remains are the seeds, the final, resistant substance of the earth. It is a land of bestial shapes twenty stories tall: black rhyolite with faces as smooth and hard as polished coral, and edges equally as sharp; bands of icy granite, white in places, peppered dark with mica and crystals; dark reds of dried blood and old roses in the steeples of andesite. Every object stands alone, worn back to original shapes that shadow the desert floor.

The sun here could evaporate over eight feet's worth of rain in a year, while only four to zero inches of rain actually fall. There is no other expanse so large in North America that receives this much sunlight in a year, these highest maximum temperatures, and this little rain. Some of these mountain ranges have not seen rain for seven years. I do not pity those who live here, though. This is their place. The balances achieved are intricate and firm: leaves that harden into thorns when they dry, urine that is delivered as crystals so that water is not lost. If the days were cool and blessed with gentle rains, most things here would die.

I turned and walked back toward our camp. Coarse seeds of granite cracked underfoot like corn in a stone mill. My body was alien in these surroundings, keeping stride with only myself, a broad-brimmed hat to keep the sun off of my head, long-sleeved shirt to cover my arms. I moved among this exhibition of huge stone forms, each a character, a story told up through the ground. As if keeping to my kind, trying not to become overwhelmed beneath these imposing objects, I thought of the jackrabbit, an animal of my own race. With veins acting as heat radiators through the lean skin of its ears, it has pursued survival through hundreds of thousands of years of genetic evolution, much as I have through my own species. It is more supple than I am, but still equally as perishable.

I came into a mile-wide tableland, the ground as pitted and ancient as an asteroid. A person of skin and blood is always a step removed from this desert, a step that we each guard obsessively, never willing to release our water to collapse lifeless on the ground, but at the same time, a step that we linger upon, wanting to know what is beyond life. I often stop myself at this point, admitting that I do not have the courage to pass any farther. I tell myself that I will walk here, that I will explore and hunt rabbits, but I will not die here.

Alerted to the lifelessness around me, my mind relayed the constant beacon that says I should turn back. This was not a welcoming place. But I had trained myself in how to move through these veils of uncertainty, reaching farther into the land.

I walked with the slingshot dangling. The ground spread in front of me, a phenomenon where each pebble and stone is driven to its flattest profile by thousands of years of wind. The space between plants (the tall and stoic saguaro cacti, the spined, sprawling arms of ocotillo, and thickets of needle-covered cholla cacti) was like the space I imagine exists between electrons—huge and barren, yet connected by unseen forces. I walked this runway until arriving at a small settlement, two backpacks and a bit of gear set here and there. I dropped my slingshot on my pack and sat down.

When Irvin returned, without a rabbit, he sat and pulled up a leg of his pants, digging something sharp from the skin of his calf with a sewing needle. He drew out the long sliver of a cactus spine. He held it up for examination. Infused with his blood, it was as transparent as rose quartz.

"Desert medicine," he said.

Soon Irvin would be leaving for seven months to study in the Dja Forest Reserve of Cameroon, then to return to the United States to become assistant manager of a national wildlife refuge near the Mexican border with California. He is a researcher, but not in any solely academic definition. With the intrepid sense of a shaman, he learns of his environment by eating insects and roots, by tattooing his skin with cactus needles. He carried with him the odd tools of his biological profession: the syringe and the alcohol vials, the book in which he could press leaves and cactus pulp, and the empty film canisters waiting to be filled with who knows what. This was not official business for him. He came with me only to walk, three weeks of crossing this uninhabited desert cache to cache.

In the evening Irvin and I ate a paltry meal of rice and posole. It was enough, in the way that after a date a quick peck on the cheek is enough. We drank water gathered three days ago at a *tinaja,* a deep hole of old, green rainwater. It tasted like a biology experiment. The chants of birds arrived as the light faded, the itching tones of cactus wrens and the subtle whines of male phainopeplas. Coveys of quail called to each other with inconsolable voices. It was as if the light, heat, and drought of the day had swallowed every movement. At twilight, life unraveled. The hidden things came out. Irvin reclined to his haunches and rolled a cigarette. A great rib cage of stars arched over us.

"I saw you this afternoon," he said, tapping ashes onto the ground.

"Where?"

He gestured off in a direction, the glow-tip of his cigarette flaring. "Out that way. I watched you for a while. You moved well, stalking that rabbit."

"I didn't kill it."

"No," he said, thinking. "No, but I like not having the meat. It makes me hungry. There's something more powerful about following these jackrabbits than killing them. It's like a ceremony we're going through, learning how the rabbit fakes and dodges, and learning how to follow it across this godforsaken place. We're being taken somewhere."

"Down the rabbit hole," I said.

He agreed, tapping his cigarette again. The smoke smelled sweet. It came from a wild species of tobacco that we had found growing in front of a cave, mildly narcotic, its leaves sticky. The leaves had dried in less than an hour, stretched like skin over the rocks.

"Do you think civilization has any use for this rabbit hole?" he asked, gesturing again to somewhere out there, his cigarette swishing toward San Diego and back to Phoenix.

I thought about this, looking in the direction of the cities, seeing nothing but heights of stone and a great, mountainous acropolis made of rhyolite, perhaps two thousand feet tall. "Maybe not," I said.

"You think we could just bulldoze and dynamite this whole place and cap it with concrete?"

"I don't think we could even get out here with a bulldozer," I said. "But I'm sure if we could, we'd take this whole place apart. We'd die off, though. We'd turn into some pale, ignorant species."

I believed even worse would happen to us if we abandoned this wilderness, and I stared out across the night desert imagining what worse could be. We would become nothing without deep and pressing country, places we can never name or possess. Our insides would weaken if we did not have such things. Our minds would become bitter and self-absorbed. I had many times tried to invent a valid argument for the preservation of wilderness and could never find it within the bounds of my language. But I knew that without these far places we were risking ourselves as a species. We need these anchors in the land. We might someday cut ourselves loose and find that there are no longer veins feeding us blood, no longer a throat to take in air. We might find that we are weak-limbed creatures unable to stand on our own.

I drew my fingers over the ground, feeling sharp little pebbles, the same kind as I had used in trying to kill the rabbit. "If we didn't have a place like this, we'd die without ever knowing we were dead," I told him. "We'd just keep building things that make our lives better, letting us live longer, but dead the whole time."

"Like ghosts," he said.

His eyes grew narrow over the pinpoint glow as he inhaled. He looked up and blew smoke into the stars.

In parched morning light, mountains stood around us, the teeth of the desert's grin. We skirted gross, black cliffs and barbed pinnacles of rock. I sat to sketch some of them as Irvin continued. They looked as if they had boiled and burned out of the planet, abandoned to fossilize from some moment when the earth spoke, when it told of its inner workings, its most principal and primordial philosophies. With a pen I drew the nearest, lowest landforms, then a small stab poking up behind it. The ink followed easily, scratching across crest and plummets. I went farther back with the pen to another set of minarets, this one with thousand-foot protrusions like emperor penguins standing in the sun. My pen moved back eight ridgelines, thirty miles out across unknown basins and huge scarps of rock. As I went, I thought that the final wealth of a place is in its landscape. Anything that I gain personally is ephemeral, easily changed or lost. The oldest stories are here, in the frozen dance of rock. What we do on the land is comparatively inquiring and temporary, throwing out beautiful nets of irrigation canals or claiming knowledge of star movements by marking points of alignment somewhere on the ground.

There are highways that streak across the outside edges of this place, blacktopped alignments of a modern age: Phoenix to Los Angeles, Tucson to San Diego, Sonoyta to San Luis Río Colorado. From them desolate stands of peaks can be seen in the distance, and behind them a haze of even farther pinnacles, which was where we were now. Sometimes I stop on the side of the road, turn the engine off, and stand there pierced by the sensation of distance. Or better yet, I have stood nowhere near a road, midday between the barren mountains of Cabeza Prieta and Tinajas Altas, my mind struggling with the heat while desiccated icebergs of granite waited around me. I have walked the craters and the dark jags of the Pinacate lava field as it barely passes from Mexico to Arizona, and the stone-encased washes of the Ajo Mountains. Inside this place sound is as rare and crystalline as water and I have turned suddenly, surprised by the rustle of wind through a dry ragweed, all of my attention focused as if the festoon of dusty-green leaves was speaking my name out loud. I have climbed the lances of the Kofa Mountains and the Trigo Mountains as the sun has set so that shadows stretched out as thin and long as pencils, giving to me a sense of how the land beneath me is shaped.

Not more than two minutes after I began drawing, losing myself in this stretch of land, Irvin shouted my name. I tied my journal closed with a strip of leather and came out from between boulders. His face appeared past a rise and he yelled something, then disappeared like an animal slipping into a hole. The only word of his that I heard was *beautiful* and the rest were lost. I scrambled through the rocks toward him.

At a slight indentation below a cliff Irvin stood with the posture of an usher. I followed his gesture to the ground where there sat a basketball-sized object with the dappled texture of an egg. I came to my knees at its boundary and wiped my hands clean on my shirt. Without weight I placed both of my palms against the object. My fingers crept over it. Its surface was a hardened, burnished clay. I lightly tapped one finger. Hollow. It was a pot.

I sat back on my haunches and looked at this thing. *People here,* I thought. There was not even a sea nearby to supply them with shell-fish, or to offer seaweed so that the water could be extracted in a solar still. I knew of these people, and had occasionally seen their artifacts. The sensation I had the day before, the gravity of Irvin walking some-where unseen, was expanded, blown up to encompass the whole of the desert. *There were others.*

A term is used for these kinds of people: *tethered nomads,* a phrase pulling two directions at once. Often they were on the move in annual cycles, but unlike agriculturists who often migrated every several generations, these people remained in their same region for thousands of years. They had come to understand their home landscape with an acute intimacy. Walking here, we frequently found evidence of their tethers, well-worn and long-abandoned trails leading to and from places of water, or a canyon floor where jojoba nuts could be gathered, or an open plain good for jackrabbits. The country is etched with these interconnected pathways, faint troughs set barely into the ground, testament to the passage of countless feet. They turn the desert into a story of ceaseless movement. The people likely had fifteen to thirty separate residences, moving between one hundred and three hundred miles in a year's time, always returning to the same places, laying their desires into the ground where we could see them and walk alongside.

The modern Mohave, descendants of these people, have been known to casually walk routes of antiquity 120 miles west to the coast of California and 350 miles northeast to the Zuni pueblo in New Mexico. This sense of motion is informed with constant purpose. The trails define the landscape in human terms, exactly how it was used and traced. I had found relevance in the pathways radiating around us, a concrete relationship with this desert that had been formed long before my arrival; lines that tell of a way of moving across the land, the most essential and incorruptible remnant of human motives. I often stopped at junctures, where paths came from great distances apart. These confluences seemed joyous and at the same time solemn. Worlds met and separated here. The land had been tied together by the every-day impressions of desert nomads.

I knew these people by the name Patayan, one of the least studied cultures in all of the Americas. I have walked their trails many times looking for water holes—*tinajas*—or just looking for a way from this place to that. I have wondered what it was that directed them. The Anasazi far to the northeast of here slipped into the sleeves and passageways leading through their canyon landscape, obeying the directions of drainages and labyrinths. The cliff dwellers below the Mogollon Rim made singular points of contact, fortresses from which all travel emanated, to which everything returned. Out here people found their guides in other ways, there being no ending or beginning to this landscape, no point to claim as here or there, only a garden of gigantic stones. To walk from these pinnacles to the Zuni pueblo is not simply a matter of finding facility in the terrain. A person must see beyond the ground. But to what? What is written in this desert beneath me?

Irvin came to the ground, the pot centered in front of us. "I almost walked by this."

"How did you see it?" I asked.

He looked down at the pot. "I don't know. It was just there."

The pot was upside down with its round butt exposed from a coarse and compact ground. A small crack, not open enough to let light in, showed along the bottom. Otherwise it was unscathed. We had no idea of its true size. We took compass bearings on it and marked its place, then began working around it with our fingers and the tips of our knives. We brushed away the debris and blew it out from around the pot. A trench formed and the vessel became larger. We fit our fingers under the lip and lifted it out on the count of three. Gingerly, we brought it from the hole, turned it right side up, and set it into a pillow we had made from the dust.

It was a big pot, forty inches around at the opening. A foot and a half deep. Rounding up from a bulbous body, the lip pouted outward. The shell was gray, charred in places from cooking. The style is known as Colorado beige, the shape putting it back to the Patayan II sequence around A.D. 1150. It was completely unadorned, no curiously shaped handles or painted geometric designs. Purely functional ware. I imagined it as a supply cache, a stock pot left hidden so far into the desert that the people had to know each turn and crag of this country like the words of an elaborate chant.

For humans to have been here seemed absurd. It is not even a place of contradiction. It is a flat-out refusal, a place that breaks life over its knee. To decipher the people who lived here through their artifacts is almost ineffective. Their personal belongings were nothing more than handy tools. An instrument is convenient as long as it does not interfere with movement. A pot is useful when it can be returned to, when it waits unbroken in the desert. What tells me more about these people than anything they manufactured or owned is the broken roll of this landscape in which they stored their belongings. This land is who they were.

Intact Patayan pot

I looked across the ceramic pot to Irvin's dark skin, at the lines of recent cuts bisecting his forearms from falling, climbing, and pushing through the brambles of catclaw and palo verde that line the dry washes. He had some good ones, scars he would bear for decades. He was rapidly becoming testimony for the land. Then I looked down at the cuts and scrapes on myself.

Carefully we filled the pot tight with dirt so that it would not readily cave in from the pressures of time. Its life span increased by maybe a few hundred years with this new packing job, for whatever that mattered. I took several sheets of paper, photocopies from an Arizona State University master's thesis on pre-Columbian populations in southwest Arizona, and covered the opening. The sheets, supported by our palms, held the packed dirt as we tilted the vessel upside down again. On the count of three we set it back into the hole and I drew out the pages one by one. We positioned the rear of the pot, matching it to our ground marks and compass bearings until we were certain that it occupied the same space it had before.

Irvin spoke a few words to the pot, to the people who left it, and to the stories around it. I had given up incantations of gratitude in English some time ago. I made a subtle bow with my head, a gesture of both inquiry and abandonment.

The pot was an anchor, an article in my mind that I carried with me as we walked. Over the weeks the desert had become littered with these points: a good place to sleep, two bobcats at the back of an arroyo, a peak shaped like the transept of a cathedral. My body stretched out the lines between each point and I wore them into grooves as I traced my memory back and forth, recalling each thing I had seen. I sometimes wondered if the ancient travel lines we were finding were not the same thing, worn by thousands of years of memory. As I traveled, I found more and more of these anchors, creating an intricate web of lines between them.

The day after finding the pot I walked alone up a narrow chine to where I would set my next anchor. The air around me was saturated with the smell of purple-flowered desert lavender and with silence stirred by my walking. I took my clothes off in the afternoon heat. And my boots. It felt good to shake free this dusty fabric. Stepping over to the solid rock wall, stones poked the arches of my feet, digging at places that usually remain hidden like love letters in a drawer. I was tantalized and pained to have them read. I backed up into the shade and stood naked against the wall. My fingers spread across the rock, searching until settling.

I looked down and saw abrasions and minor, swollen infections from cactus spines in my skin. I saw wholesale pieces of flesh missing, the tears covered with cornflake scabs. What a raw creature this body is, I thought. A tool. The thing I use to get into the deepest wilderness. Now it has brought me here. I looked up from my skin and I saw the desert.

My mind instantly dissolved into the terrain. I felt as if I was losing consciousness, but my eyes were still open. The beast who lives in my skin changed color. My eyes camouflaged themselves, matching the rock behind me. I knew all along that it was my own body, and that I could stand away from the wall on my own volition at any moment and take my color back. But I did not stand away. I had at my disposal the ability to observe, to remain apart, but for this moment the veil vanished. I was aware of a notebook in my pocket in a lump of clothes nearby. There would be nothing to write in that notebook. A sweet, forever emptiness consumed me, stretching beyond this wall into the infinite desert to all directions. I suddenly thought that if Irvin walked by he would not be able to see me. Life would rush into my muscles. I would lunge for his throat.

I did not attack Irvin. When I saw him next he was sitting in camp with a dry animal bone in his hand, studying it as if expecting it to soon come to life. I had put clothes back on, and my skin was now the expected, tanned color of a biscuit, my eyes again blue. I did not mention to him this brief, naked flight.

Later in the day we traveled south together, the land around us as rough and incongruous as the stone of an apricot. I walked with the weight of my pack, thinking of the morning's event. It was there, against the rock, that I felt that there is no boundary to the soul. Like seeing the night sky pressed with stars, it had been a sensation both fascinating with depth and terrifying in its emptiness. The hunting and gathering people who lived here must have been this close. How fragile life must have seemed to them. To be alive here, to not be called away, is a rare and marvelous feat.

Two days after finding the pot we stopped late in the day and sat for a while to rest. The land was open around us, high tips of rock in the distance carved like glacial arêtes, places that had never seen ice.

We had been taking a couple hours each afternoon in search of jackrabbits. Any conceit we once had about hunting was long gone. We enjoyed the hunt and the attentiveness it required as we walked, even if we never neared or even saw a jackrabbit. At the end of our days we talked of the artifacts we had discovered: stone hunting weapons on the ground, the pot with its suggestion of cooking and life, and the threads of trails vanishing over thousands of years. We talked about the hunting, the fact that we could have netted a few birds while we walked, or stabbed a snake and cooked it over a fire, but we were concentrated on the jackrabbit alone, learning everything we could about how it moves and how it sees the world. We learned to become the jackrabbit, taking its leaps and strides into our breath. We agreed that it would not have been possible to kill another kind of animal while on this hunt.

Sitting against our packs, we both saw motion. A jackrabbit stopped at a rise on our periphery. Its ears stood straight up as if receiving radio waves. Without words we grabbed our slingshots and slid off in opposite directions, circling around on the animal. I took the slow, quiet approach toward its head while Irvin came around to catch it from behind, preparing for it to turn and run from me. When I reached the point where I could clearly see the brown ring of its eyes, energy transferred into its hind legs.

A quarter-second before it could run, I shot a small rock into its front leg. It tumbled into the dirt, skidding, leg broken. Just as I leapt forward, it was gone, regaining most of its speed.

I ran behind it, slipping another rock into the slingshot. I tried to keep my eye on its body, my arms steady as I bounded. Don't lose aim. See nothing but the rabbit. I felt a cord between me and it. I did not let this cord go slack or become so stretched it might snap. The black tail in front of me was as dark and short as a comma. I could smell the rabbit's escape scent, a sharp musk quick to my nose. The rabbit was throwing variables at me, trying to load me with too much information, gaining the eighth-of-a-second advantage it might need to escape.

My rock flew and hit. A hollow thud, the breaking of ribs. The rabbit rolled like a ball, but picked up again, down through bursage bushes toward a low arroyo, a panicked blur of motion. If I could keep it in the wash-sand of the arroyo, it would not be able to gather much speed. Irvin kept to the outside, ready for it to dart toward him. It tried the customary rabbit tricks, faking its directions, but in the flying dust between two attackers, it could not get away. The jackrabbit and I nearly slid into each other. The rabbit toppled, scrambling to get back up. When our eyes met, the rabbit on its side looking up at me, there was a very brief conversation.

I have you, I said.

I know, the jackrabbit told me.

Before I could shoot again, the jackrabbit slipped beneath a creosote, not willing to yield so quickly. I jumped through the branches to meet it on the other side. There was motion from outside of our perimeter, something small and fast flying at both of us. Suddenly one of the powerful hind legs shattered out from under the rabbit. A fist-sized rock skittered away. I saw Irvin, his body recoiling from a throw, his slingshot dropped on the ground behind him. The rabbit was stunned. I could grab it with my hands now. My slingshot fell and my hands were free.

I had killed and eaten rabbits before, but I had been a child and a teenager then, and I had used a gun. The killing had always been done at a shooting distance, the animal fixed on the front and rear sights along my barrel, and always motionless by the time I reached it, its eyes glassed in absence. Each time I had killed one, I knelt beside it and placed my hand on its body, feeling the warmth of its escaping life.

This time I came to the jackrabbit and it was still very much alive. Its eyes were full of terror. There were a hundred questions in my head, but they could not be answered. Not now. I placed my boot sole against the rabbit's body and took its head in my right hand. Settling it squarely in my palm, I pulled quickly. The jackrabbit's spine snapped. Legs kicked as nerves drew back to the most core impulse: *Live.*

The jackrabbit died, although it took some time and we both worried that we had not done this properly. We both stood over it when it was finally still, relieved, but somehow disquieted. Irvin and I had come from a different society than that of the rabbit. We had no native way of reconciling death with life, violence with custom. Our culture wraps death in distracting, ambiguous packaging—slabs of red meat in grocery store cellophane, or crisply brown out of the oven. A person no longer needs understand a creature to be involved in its death.

The jackrabbit's eyes lost their sharpness. I knelt and ran a curious, admiring hand into its fur, feeling the warmth. I still wanted to know more about the rabbit. I wanted to take in its life here in the desert. I spread my fingers on its body.

"Okay," Irvin said, his voice nervous. "We've killed an animal here. This is important. How are we going to do this?"

"We carry it back, clean it, and take it somewhere to cook it."

"I mean, we've killed something. This rabbit was alive here."

"I know," I said. "I know."

I thought of a coyote I had seen days before, trotting away with a jackrabbit clutched in its mouth, moving through the desert. There are paths taken here, the same way time and again, lines set down in the land. The society of living and dying, I thought, is far more complex and rich than my own so-called civilized world. There is so much more here. Irvin and I were only now learning, changing ourselves into desert minds, following the *tinajas,* the kill, the cache, the walk, the silent reverence, and the constant metamorphosis. *We've killed something,* I told myself.

We walked toward our packs. In my right hand I carried the jackrabbit by its hind legs. The slack body strung out easily, so different now, relieved of itself. I was careful not to let the ears drag on the ground.

At our packs Irvin cut away the skin with precise, fluid motions. With a small knife and his fingers he worked beneath the flesh and pulled it free. He fished into the body cavity with his hands. He slipped his knife in, a serrated knife he once used on a fishing boat in Alaska. There was a scissoring motion with the fabric-cut of muscles coming free. He pulled out the heart and dropped it into my hand. It was warm and tense to the touch. I held it up, a gnome cap of muscle. This is life, I thought, indulgent and beautifully excessive. We are each discrete containers of life in this desert, guarding our water and our blood, moving around in a state of astonishment and alertness, leaving and falling into pathways wherever we go. Blood came down my fingers, snake curves working around my wrist.

We loaded the butchered rabbit into my pack. The entrails, head, and skin were left beneath a chuparosa bush where earlier we had spied a sleeping coyote. An offering. We hiked southwest with our gear and the meat, aiming for a rocky knob where we could get up high and prepare a feast.

The point of rocks had a good view of the surrounding land. We hoisted gear to a slight alcove on its eastern face. There we found two Patayan grinding holes polished into the rock. Jojoba nuts and mesquite seeds had once been ground into meal here, a task repeated for generations until the holes were left deep and smooth. A good place for a meal. We marinated the rabbit in wild mustard, desert lavender, salt, and blood. In the early evening we cooked it on a hot fire of ironwood and palo verde branches, setting the rabbit directly on the coals.

As each piece was ready, first the legs, then the back, we pulled it out. The meat was tough, strong, and tasted good. There was ample food, more than we imagined a single rabbit would offer. We peeled it out with our fingertips and our teeth as we recounted the events of the past few days. We threw the bones back into the fire.

Into the night we poked the shrunken fire with sticks, commenting on the flavor of the rabbit long after we had finished, and on having so much food in our bodies. We were sluggish, standing only to fetch more wood. The fire had become mostly coals. Finally, neither of us wanted to get up for more wood. The hot pit of dim shapes grew brighter as we leaned forward and blew across them. Our faces were the only objects lit, turned a glowing pumpkin orange.

To occupy our hands, we drew the diminutive bones out of the coals with sticks. The bones were fragile now and some broke to the touch. The fire had altered their properties like cooked ceramics. The fibrous interiors were black, while the outsides turned a ghostly, calcine white.

In caves around here, once used by the Patayan, we had found the same thing—burned rabbit bones in ash. With the bones were shards of pottery, the remains of other, older banquets. These antique rabbit bones had been equally as fragile hundreds and thousands of years ago, perhaps gathered out of the ashes in the same after-dinner ritual of indolence.

A few archaeologists had studied the burned bones of the south-western desert and in some cases they found those of numerous large animals, bighorn sheep or Sonoran pronghorn, and in certain instances, burned mounds of nothing but jackrabbit. Modern tribes not far from here still recall this practice of eating animals and ritual-istically burning their remains. A few of the Tohono O'odham, recall-ing their own rituals of bone-burning in the desert east of here, have suggested that with this act people were clearing the air between the hunter and the hunted. These ash-colored heaps around the desert are mile markers noting the acquisition of balance and sustenance. They are part of a ceremony, like saying grace before supper, like lighting candles at a vigil. An act is performed, a pathway set between the ancient triad of the animal, the hunter, and the desert.

Irvin and I had fallen into the ritual. This was as close as I could come to describing the Patayan to myself, stepping into their line of travel across this hard country as if by custom of the place. As we arranged the bones, they clinked like tiny crystal chimes. We moved them around on the rocks, making piles, listening to their different tones. They had surrendered to the law of this spare desert where the only thing still divisible is life. The wise and fast jackrabbit had undergone a final transformation. Its once strong bones had turned to glass.

LAVA

Volcán Santa Clara, Sonora, Mexico

All that is left is this. Rock. Everywhere, rock. Black as India ink. And a strong wind that sings across the smallest volcanic jag. Miles upon miles of rock and desert wind. Nothing in motion except for me, a figure dropping in and out, rising to a crest then down.

Every step came calculated, the weight on my back mostly water, my boots losing thin curls of leather to the crevices. Moving any quicker than with mincing steps was mentally taxing and physically exhausting, so I remained slow. To get a vantage I climbed a stony hook of lava to a tall, angled slab. It was something that looked as if it had been caught sinking, its bow lifted skyward, pearls of shiny black rock dripping beneath. I gathered myself at its top like a waiting bird.

The earth here is scraped down so far that the molten interior has come bursting out. Volcanoes turned dormant only recently stood all around me, and between these were tumbled fields of lava; great exploded arms welded together, not a single flat place to sit. No boulders or individual rocks, this was a one-piece land, a dark sea. There was no end that I could see. One saguaro stood a couple miles away. It had no arms, just a single pillar of green shrouded in needles. It seemed out of place and I felt for a moment that I should walk to it. I should stay there beneath it, crouched in its single stab of shade, conferring with it out of respect. But that was not my destination.

I was walking down on a solo trek from range to range in the Sonoran Desert, finally arriving here in Mexico where the desert turned black. I had passed from a country of craggy peaks to this place, newborn terrain with shapes more ancient than anything I had seen before. What I found was a strange sense of equanimity. No single shape of rock or depression was easily distinguishable from another, yet to my eyes they each were utterly dissimilar, thrown and poured in different ways.

I looked out from my perch. Cinder cones lifted in front of a barren volcano at the horizon, the place called Volcán Santa Clara that was my destination. No direction of travel seemed any better than another. My eyes struggled for some pattern, a guide to follow. There was none. I saw currents and crosscurrents in the once-fluid rock. Whirlpools sat frozen, surrounded by waves of black, hard cake batter. Fossilized ropes bunched against each other.

It is alive, I thought. I listened to myself breathe as I thought this. Not life in the way I would imagine. It is alive in the way that water is alive, filled with direction and intention. The wealth of shapes plagued my eyes, so much happening all at once, frozen in this moment so that I could walk across the surface of creation and destruction without them rising to strangle me.

I brought out a pair of binoculars and scanned the distance. Lava had once poured off the flanks of the Santa Clara shield volcano, crossing the desert nearly thirty miles north toward what is now Arizona, twenty miles south, and thirty miles east to west, studded here and there with new, smaller volcanoes, and sudden gasps from the pit of the earth that had left peaks of cinders. In the sidewalls of these cinder cones, vents opened straight from below where the lava had once welled upward, leaving drapes and mobs of rock. I moved the binoculars up to the cones, studying their shapes, hoping to see a steep arroyo that might house a water hole. It was not the right kind of place at all for water, not the right kind of rock. I dropped the binoculars onto my thighs. If there were no arroyos, where would there be water?

The landscape seemed to give me nothing. I could not even see a way to walk. There were no arroyos or ridges to follow, no canyons with sheltering walls. It looked like the breaking of spring river ice, enormous tablets thrown into each other, ingots lying about, half-melted back into the earth.

The last water hole I had used was back in Arizona days ago, in the smooth, white granite of a canyon that at the time felt desolate, and now seemed like paradise. The water had been dark with age, its surface laced with dead moths. It tasted of death. Each time I had walked away from one of these water holes into the unknown desert ahead, I had the nervous sensation of a free fall. I did not know where I would land next.

I could not land here. This was the crossing of the barren. I had to reach the other side. I let the thought of water go and instead focused on where to walk next. Normally I would come to the top of a prominence and no matter how preposterous the terrain, reach some conclusion. I would pick a course, even if only a random gesture. But there was no pathway here. I aligned myself with the farthest volcano and climbed down, heading in its direction, beating against the shape of the land.

Since entering the lava field I had seen no sign of people. There were no airplanes dragging their contrails around the sky. Even the faint thousand-year-old trails of the Patayan had vanished, leaving nothing to govern this vastness for me.

I hunted for a piece of pottery or a broken stone tool and the only thing I found was the brilliant white flower of sacred datura, its petals sagging like a hang-dried cloth. I crouched and rubbed its dark green leaves between my thumb and forefinger, smelling the dark, musty scent of its poisons. It is a plant so strong that eating a few of its seeds would bring violent hallucinations and maybe death a drug-induced way, I have heard, of seeing beyond the fragile limits of the mind. This was one of the only living things I could find, and not a scrap of human presence.

I had always followed the signs of ancient people because I did not want to be in a place where I did not belong. They would have known which corners of the earth to avoid. Where was I now?

By dark I had gained no more than four miles. I camped in a clutch of lava, sitting in plain view of the sky. With me were some papers by

Julian Hayden, an archaeologist who loved this place, a man who drove his International Travelall out to the edges of these rock fields up until his death. He had made 150 trips into these craters and lava flows, looking for what? The same thing I am here for perhaps, reaching for the interior of the planet in hopes someone was once here to leave a sign.

I used his journal articles as a cushion where I sat. I spoke with him out loud, gesturing as I conversed. He had died some years earlier, and his ashes were scattered here, so I at least felt sane in talking to him. At first I had asked him questions, starting a couple of days ago.

Where's the water, Julian? May I call you Julian? How did you get across this lava field? What did you do with your mind? Oh, forget it. Just tell me where the water is. And these artifacts you found, did you have some obsessive love for the people who lived here? Was it because they knew only this . . . this place? Because they were made of infinite generations as far as they could know, each mind strung through this crazy land and through time like thread through a needle? Oh yeah, just stick to water. Thanks. Where is it? A day from here? Two? I need to know.

Still a few days from my next supply, my dinner was peanuts, eight dried figs, some almonds, and fresh coconut that was becoming less and less fresh. I pulled Julian's papers out from under my butt. I laid back on the ground, inserting them beneath my shoulder blades. I looked through the stars, into the deep velvet blue behind them.

I don't know, Julian. Maybe it's something about this place. Did you ever get tired of it on top of you day and night? I mean, there's no rest here. It pulls your soul inside out. Sort of a dry washing machine and you're never clean until you've turned to sand and wind.

I rearranged his papers, softening the ground. I let my eyes wander.

You think humans should go this far? Sure, you do. You found one of their pots out here, right? It was completely intact. You found it in the sand out west of those cinder cones. I remember. I saw a picture of it, a little neck so that it wouldn't lose the water it was supposed to hold. It was proof for you that they were here, right? But then, maybe they weren't human. Not in the way we think, at least. They were perfect. Is that how you see it? Perfect?

No answer. Of course. I closed my eyes, thinking of perfection, of a person stripped by the land until there is nothing left but the raw, honest soul. I fell asleep, the desert huge around me.

Days? How many? Does it matter? These drifting miles distorted my sense of time, the length of the day becoming greater and greater, while by nightfall my day seemed to have been sudden, a flash of sun across my memory. I walked through troughs and ridges of lava with an insomniac's fatal stare, woken occasionally by a bowl of fine black cinders; the white skeleton of a plant; a hawk swaying into view, then skating over the ridge of a hundred-foot-tall lava swell, wings seesawing in the heat breezes.

The hunger for food rose through me. The thirst for water curled up like a dusty animal in my mouth, my tongue swollen. A dry catchnet of phlegm spun across the back of my throat, constantly plucking at my attention. I rationed myself to just over half a quart of water per day, which teased my eyes with mild hallucinations and sparks of unexpected light.

Cinders crushed in gravelly tones beneath my boots. I had the haunting feeling that I was leaving a trail of drops as I moved across the desert. Drops of what? Water, blood, life? I imagined that the drops were falling onto rocks and into the black crags. Half believing this, I stopped to look back and see if it was true, if I was indeed bleeding on the ground. Just in case. When I turned around, the lava field behind me spread like an ocean and I could not see the trail of blood I'd been leaving. There was too much topography, no real ground to focus my eyes. I just stared.

I felt the day's heat rising from the black rock, shivering the hair on my forearms, brushing my face. I was being read. The world studied me as I studied it back.

Is there no separation between us?

My body was stripped down, my mind robbed defenseless. I kept walking, looking as I went for a sign of humans to ease the loneliness, but I found none of this. A trail would have told me stories. Broken pottery would have brought me back into time. But I found none of this. I came here estranged from humanity, wondering how it was done before me, how the hunters and water-seekers had crossed these limitless barrens.

For this moment I wished that I could speak with those who had lived here, passing the barriers of time, language, and culture. I would ask if there was a ceremony for walking the desert, some way of seeing that helps with this growing sense of endlessness. Is this where religion began, where someone first spoke the name of God not as a way to get through, but to speak of something witnessed here?

As I walked, I went back into my mind, setting mental anchors for myself, thoughts that I could hang on to. Cultures had taught me of subtle trails and cliff dwellings. I had been sent by them to massive gorges, to slender canyons, to the low, broken country, and to here, where the paths finally faded and I was left alone. I thought of Kim Malville the archaeoastronomer and George Steck the mathematician, the two wise men of the canyon deserts leading me into the symmetry and repetition of the landscape. I thought of Laura Slavik and her fierceness, the Patayan and their ceaseless movement. Regan Choi, teacher of grace and observance. The cliff dwellers of the Mogollon Rim telling me how to seek protection in wild country.

Here they left me, a madman in the barrens, light streaking around me, the sky clean of clouds. I no longer chose where to walk or what to believe. I had no idea if I was revealed or ruined, if my travels were a mark of escapism or the direct route into the heart. I stepped up to the top of a broken-down fence of lava and crouched to take the weight of my pack down to my legs. I stayed there looking around, not so much to find a way, but to put a punctuation mark into the day, a place to distinguish one moment from the next and arrest this inexorable flow.

Late in the day I reached the edge of the lava flow. It was like stepping off of a storm-pitched ship onto solid ground. But I seemed to be no nearer or farther from anything. In fact, I had foolishly hoped to find an oasis here at the end of the lava. I quickly realized where I was, that no lakes were going to suddenly appear. I tested the dry and unvaried floor, climbing off of a fat roll of lava, planting my boot soles, shifting my weight. I walked onto a clear, black plain. I could have run had I wanted. I could have flown. The earth was as smooth as ground glass, composed of countless tiny stones reflecting the sky for miles. This mirror took on chromatic tones as I walked with dusk sailing over my head. The ground glowed, reflecting the last light, then turned blue, then dark. I unloaded my gear for the night, sitting on the sky.

There were no airplanes overhead, although I hunted for them, hoping to see one. This was off-route to everywhere, leaving me with only the incautious trails of satellites, unblinking points of light moving steadily against the grain of stars. We were the sole human presence down here, I thought: me, the satellites, and Julian Hayden's ghost.

Pulling the last quarter of a coconut from a plastic bag, I slipped the edge of my knife blade between its wood shell and the snowy flesh. I smelled mold. The coconut had been hot in my pack and had gone fuzzy during the day. It was now inedible. I should not have kept it in plastic. I reminded myself to be careful and not to make any more small mistakes, not this far into the desert.

I put the coconut aside and reached for another bag, fumbling with its twist tie for a moment, confounded by which way to unwind it, staring at it, then staring at my fingers. My fingers seemed old and cracked, and I thought that if I was too clumsy with them, they might fall apart, dry as wallboard. After a while I lifted my head, letting my attention slowly shift from my fingers, arriving at a shape in the distance, a stranded chunk of lava. I heard a breeze behind me humming through a creosote bush and I tried to follow it in my imagination, wondering if it would come to me, if it would move across my skin. It didn't. I looked down and saw the twist tie still between my fingers. *Open the bag,* I told myself.

Inside I found seventeen almonds and four dried figs. This was all the food I had left. I counted twice. It would be two days until a resupply, when I would meet Regan on a Mexican back road. This food needed to last until then. I had made an error in my food calculations. How many days ago had I made this error? When had I eaten more than my day's share? I took four almonds for the night and saved the rest for the next morning. I would need their energy in searching for water.

Chewing slowly on the almonds, I closed the bags and pushed them around to my back where I could not see them. My muscles sank into me, reserving their strength. I felt clean and firm as a tuning fork planted in the desert, waiting to be struck, dying for even the slightest vibration.

I drew the notebook from my shirt pocket and scratched at it with a pen.

I am aware of my mortality as if it were a fire out of control. I feed off of it. Off this contrast. The brief and the forever. I am a meteoric creature crossing through the infinite. What kind of crazy ecstasy is this? I am the knowledge of passing stars and the perpetual memory of stone. At the same time I am a fragile weave of muscles and blood, something that will die, something filled with fear and weakness. And what is this place that I come to? It is desire. It is the urge I feel to live and to die. It is the shape that uncoils around me, filled with vigor and longing. The lava, the sky, the distance, the stones on the ground. There is a drive embedded into everything, no matter how still or how quick. When the world is boiled down, when we tear through the layers and cords, there is only this, the inside of wilderness, the single instruction given to the universe. Desire.

I held onto my writing as long as I could, but it dissolved. I became aware of the desert again. Its fullness turned into a manifestation, something that did not begin or end at my body. It was the very heart of the beast, its voice distilled into an acid that saturated the air, burning through me, carving open my organs.

All this time I had thought that the land was something other than me, something I sensed as if I had feelers dancing across it. Now I could see. We had the same command, driven by the same fundamental longing. I had never been a separate creature from it, not once. All this time I believed that I had my own desires, my own hands. Laughable, now. I have always been the land.

My pen hovered above the paper and I could not remember my thoughts. It was hunger and thirst, I figured, stealing what was left of my mind. The words I'd written seemed vain and fleeting now that they were in black ink. Perhaps this was what people who once lived here understood: there can be nothing but desire, otherwise a person might sit in this black infinity and never move again.

Enough clever thinking. I felt angry for trying to capture the sensation of this illimitable desert. It was as if I were suspicious, trying to detect words where there were none. This sense of longing that I tried to write about, even using the word *desire,* tore it from me, rendering its power, turning it into a thought, a weapon, something other than what it is. There is a greater sense in this desert that I could never write. It is the very root of existence, the thing that is beyond beauty and safety, beyond need.

I closed the notebook and set it on the ground, pen marking the spot where I had left off. Then I pulled the pen out, losing my place, withdrawing the temptation to write. I tossed it and it landed ten feet away, clattering mechanically among the rocks. That is how a pen should write, I thought, with no fingers touching it.

I stared at where it had landed, rubbing the smooth, hard callus from the pen on my middle-right finger.

Closer to me I saw a lighter. It was within reach. I should use it, I thought, and set fire to this useless notebook. It would ignite easily, starting at its flimsy cardboard cover, burning through 150 pages, leaving only the tight metal spiral discolored from the heat. Then my words would no longer be bound and inadequate. Thousands of verbs and adjectives would finally be free, flying away with the smoke.

When I looked at the ground even nearer, I saw the knife I had used on the coconut. I picked it up, studying its blade. I brought it flat to my lips. The steel was not cold.

Fire could free the words in my notebook just like this knife could free me. If I were to cut my tongue, I thought, sever it completely, then I would silence the weaknesses of my voice. Without my tongue I would never speak, never try to reduce this landscape to something conceivable. I would close off this avenue of escape from the desert, becoming even more a creature of the land.

A warning signal fired from within my head. I would claw the ground in pain if I did this. I would bleed to death. But even that seemed acceptable in these dazzling stages of thirst and hunger. I would no longer be mortal, I thought. I would lie dead, a feast for the wind. This must be the madness that overtakes people who die in the desert, the strange final acts of suicides, the last precious water poured deliriously onto the ground. I touched the edge of the blade with my tongue. My fatigue will act as anesthesia, I thought.

The sharpness of the knife slid to the base of my tongue, still curious, not yet cutting flesh. I should take one more step, I thought. The land pulled on me, a magnet to steel, the poison of a snake entering the blood of a small animal. *Come,* it said. *Yes, come.*

A woman came to mind, a friend who once, under the tutelage of a shaman, ate a poisonous peyote cactus and saw through the eyes of a raven. In a trance of sensations, she found that her arms were draped neatly with black feathers. Later, after vomiting and scratching at the air, she saw herself in a wolf's body, her four legs striking ground.

Instead of the blinding heat of her hallucinogenic cactus, I now had rocks and sky in my blood. Is this what she had experienced, I wondered. She was a scientist who studied animals, who examined their organs and bones in the lab, bloodying herself with their beauty. Animals were her fascination. If she became an animal, I thought, will I become the land?

I studied the soft flesh under my tongue with the knife. Still curious. Not yet . . .

I remembered again the desire I had written about in my notebook, the thing that I had wanted to free, the pages I had wanted to burn. Desire means nothing without a body, I told myself, holding back just enough so that the blade would not draw blood.

I thought that words must be formed by a voice, by a pen on paper. Wilderness must take a form. What is it that the land has taught me? To be bound and unbound at once. To be seamlessly mortal and infinite. To live.

Slowly, I withdrew the knife, staring over this darkening country. As the knife came down, the desert changed. It spread around me the way circles of water ripple outward when a stone has dropped into the center. I fanned into the land, rippling across the surface in all directions. I could smell the ground, its dark volcanic dust driven into crannies and protected beneath mats of stone. I felt the shape of every crag. At that moment I realized that I had fed my life to the land. But I was not dead. I was still here, amazed as I took in a breath, the air as palpable as water through my lungs.

I had no sense of size, sitting here. No distance or time. Not one thing could be separated or compared to another to give me a vantage. The stones, the horizon, my body, these could not be broken down any farther. My life had given me moments here and there, flashes of awareness upon the sudden passing of birds, upon an enchanting quality of light, or the up-close stare of a mountain lion, but never such sustained awakening as this. I no longer felt my body or my bones. Like an animal finally dead, I stopped scratching and fighting. The last of my muscles gave way. I felt my hand falling under the weight of the knife.

After a while . . . how many hours? . . . a thought came to me, up from far-off memory. Regan. Her name formed into my mind. There was a love letter from her in my pocket, the paper as folded and soft as an old map. I became aware of this letter, the exact words on it, the cursive of her signature. She would be here in only two days. She would bring water and food. Her hair would be smooth and her skin would smell of freshness and life.

The first thought of another person seemed to clear a space in front of me. I saw in my right hand the knife. I hefted it slowly, testing its weight as if it had just been placed there. On the ground was my notebook and some of my gear. The notebook was unharmed. A pen rested among rocks farther out. Then the long, black tapestry of desert pavement, a rise and fall to the terrain. I saw the dry night sky, the stars not even trembling. It was as if I was coming out of a sound sleep, which caused the moon to be strangely crisp, burning its way through the darkness.

A skull rested on the ground. I could tell by its curve, by the bleached white glowing against the sun, that it was the half-buried skull of a Sonoran pronghorn or perhaps a coyote, a sign of life. I walked to it on my morning search for water, my pack light and easy to carry. I crossed the plain to where I came to a crouch and picked it up. It was not a skull. The roundness had tricked me and now I held a seashell deep as a salad bowl. One side of its bivalve hinge was still intact, coiled ornately like the neck of a violin.

The ground suddenly jumped alive to my eyes. If there was a shell, there would have been people.

The Sea of Cortés, west of here, had been the source of most prehistoric trade shells in the Southwest, so there must have been a route through here.

Realizing this, I put the shell back and came down to all fours. I lowered my head the way a dog scents on the ground. Scanning around me I immediately saw a trail. It was muted, barely visible, hundreds, thousands of years old. I crawled to it only a few feet away and set my hand into its meager depression, a place where feet had once come through, where the Patayan had been. Even my hand could hardly find it, the ground bowing inward maybe a quarter of an inch, just deep enough to alter its shade of light.

There would be a route to follow. There would be water. *I am not alone,* I thought.

I sat back onto the ground, calibrating my vision to the faintness of this trail, following it with my eyes, hands motionless in my lap. Other lines of travel joined this one, stretching across the ground. In the heat, both numbing and alerting at once, a cipher of tracks spread around me; faded, ghostly paths. People once traveled along the margin of this lava field, arriving from great distances, living at the sharp edge of human life. I slowly turned my head, then shifted my body to see all around me. These obscure streaks headed off to all points: ways for a person to live written across the ground as articulate as any story or address I had ever listened to.

To the earliest travelers each path had significance: one quicker from here to there, one a better vantage for hunting, one to guaranteed water, one passing near to shelter. To my novice eyes, they were little more than stray lines going nowhere. I studied them imagining the one to guaranteed water. There must be more than invention to my travels here, I thought, more than the wit of telling a story. Choosing one of the lines, I stood.

I moved slowly, losing it for twenty yards, getting it back. Ten minutes later, I came upon broken pottery in a bowl of wind-driven sand. I bent down to examine this, a Patayan pot that had been smashed into fourteen pieces, rusty orange on the inside, gray on the outside. Then, not far beyond the pottery, was a grinding stone, a plain metate polished smooth.

Once the trail was fixed into my eyes, I had no trouble staying with it, finding broken white curves of shells and little triangles of abandoned ceramics all over. To my right an arroyo dug beneath the surface, cutting a slight canyon for itself into the basalt. The trail entered it. Wild tobacco grew along the edges with leaves a startling green. There was a palo verde tree, then an ironwood, each invisible from the concealing land up top. Bees hungrily overtook the tiny flowers of desert lavender. I walked into a cavern in the basalt. In the back was a *tinaja* cradling hundreds of gallons of clear water.

I slid from my pack, letting it drop. There were bird feathers on the ground. Those of white-tailed doves were creamy gray, gilded flickers a reddish orange, and the phainopeplas transparent black. Tracks of animals pushed their way into damp sand. A coyote. A pronghorn. A small cat, even. The landscape was not as it had first appeared. From a hundred yards away this low canyon had been invisible, below the general horizon. There had been no water, no animal, no life. Then here a band of tiny, chattering warblers descended through the branches of a mesquite tree, fiercely scolding me.

I came to the edge of the *tinaja* and slid my hand inside. Cold, cold water. Within was a refuge of tiny creatures swimming between one another, panicked with life. Placing my palms in the sand, I leaned over and drank.

Water boatman patrolling a tinaja

EPILOGUE

The Sand

Down the flanks of the volcano stand cinder cones and cornices of lava. I sit high in this mound of rock, staring at a single dirt road below. The road goes on as far as I can see, so that I can know twenty miles ahead of time if a vehicle comes along. I wait for Regan, for the squeak and growl of our truck's suspension over grades and rocks. Distant dust devils take the place of her approach every now and then. Through hours I wait, sitting still as the day shifts, the shadows of saguaros methodically leaning toward evening. I had found the water I needed the morning before, but now I am deeply hungry. The hunger feels clean, like waking up empty, ready to eat. I am an empty pot, waiting.

When the truck does appear, when dust follows it for miles and I finally hear the sound—the alien stress of metal and gears broadcast through the air—I dive off the backside of my perch. With my gear banging against me, I run eight hundred feet down through boulders and crooked faces of lava, into corridors of eroded magma tubes, over platforms of freshly laid volcanic rock as delicate as Japanese fans. I want to reach the road before Regan. I want to catch my breath and unload my gear in a casual manner, so it will not appear as if I had been watching for her all day, letting my excitement rise and fall with every dust devil.

At the road I tip my pack upside down and unload a small hermit's camp onto the ground. I arrange everything, pulling out small gifts and letters I had written to her while I was out. The truck arrives half an hour later. The engine turns off, ticking as it loses its heat. When Regan steps out, I stare from twenty feet away, then approach her. The sharpness of another life seems unlikely here, unexpected. She is a person of emotion, a flame as real as my own. We walk to each other and fall into each other's arms. I inhale this feeling, the warmth of her skin, her tongue, the scent at the back of her neck rich with sweat and something familiar that I cannot name.

She had brought a dozen red roses from Arizona, and a fringe of baby's breath, all tied together with a broad, red ribbon. I recognize her hand in the knot. The thorns graze my fingers as she passes the flowers to me. I smell them gratefully. Then she gives to me a small bundle that she had gathered during her recent travels in a more hospitable part of the desert northeast of here. It is a swatch of white lace containing a handful of fresh jojoba nuts, kept closed with a narrow, red ribbon. She gives it with no explanation.

This is how we tell stories to each other. Gestures and suggestions. Nothing is lost between us. I hand her a circle of shells, little cowries and pieces of scallop tied together with fishing line, each item gathered by me from the Sea of Cortés not long ago.

In the last light I brush her hair as she sits with bare feet on hard, black cinders. Like dark water, her hair threads through my hands, down below the middle of her back. "I want to see everything," she says as I brush. "Tell me what you've found out here."

I tell her of the frustration of crossing the lava field, of running low on food and water, and of finding a flower of the sacred datura plant, soft as linen. I tell her of a strange night when I touched the thing that I always believed I would find, when I came down to the core of my life and found there nothing but desire, the truth of the land. I say that it was her name that came to me on that night, causing me to lift my head and wake as if from a dream.

She smiles at all of this. The knowing, inward smile of my wife, reaching out to touch me. She is glad that I have returned to her, stepping from that world back to this one. I tell her, as emphatic as a child, that I had not come back. I am still there. I had learned the truth of the desert. I had been changed. She nods her head and turns to kiss me. Her eyes say, of course. I know you have changed. Love me.

The next morning Regan and I walk around the southeast skirt of the volcano. The air is hot by ten o'clock. We take to the boulder shade of a canyon and sit to rest. She brushes sweat from her forehead. The canyon smells of rock dust, chuparosa flowers, and the astringent leaves and bark of a nearby elephant tree. She says nothing, just breathes quietly, pulling a small tangerine from her pack. As she unwinds the rind from the flesh, the scent of the canyon completely changes. I watch each move of hers, inhaling this new tangerine smell, the biting sweetness of fresh citrus. What a strange thing out here, like a ruby in the sand, like the smell of rain.

By early afternoon we round even farther southeast, the slope of the volcano boulder-covered and stippled with saguaro cacti. There we come across a rock shrine, work of the Patayan, several hundred dictionary-sized rocks placed into a cone five feet tall, the same shape of the overshadowing volcano. I crouch before the shrine, studying its symmetrical shape, the placement of its stones. People had made an intentional mark, not the habit of a trail or the accidents of broken artifacts or dropped shells. I look up at her from my crouch and smile. They had been here.

Less than half a mile away is a single line of rocks, each the same size as those composing the shrine. The line had been constructed by human hands due north to due south, just over one hundred feet in length with no apparent function. Farther out from this line is a scattering of broken shells, pottery, and stacked-rock wind shelters. We try the shelters, curling into their protective horseshoe shapes, just tall enough so that our highest points, our shoulders, are blocked from a southern wind.

Signs of people accumulate around us, as if we were walking into a welcoming crowd. There are hundreds of broken seashells and the remains of numerous pots. When we divide, Regan curling for a nap on the ground below five young saguaros, and me off to find more of these rock designs, I come upon about a hundred rays of stone lines. They all neatly follow each other side by side, and are angled enough so that they leave from a center point in the west and spread to all directions east. I stand in this array and look around, seeing how the rocks are each beginning to cast evening shadows, feeling again this sense of strange companionship, as if I had been returned to the people.

Many had been here, recording on the ground something ceremonial, some story, or a calendar to be read against celestial motions. Perhaps it was the lunatics who built these things, who put themselves to work arranging stones. There are more stones in this desert than there are leaves in a forest. There is no end to the possible arrangements, rocks positioned in lines pointing toward the rising stars, to cycles of the moon nearly two decades long, to the solstice sunrise of winter, or to nowhere in particular.

Every rock that the Patayan had moved is exactly where they had left it, the topside black and polished from exposure to the environment, the underside as rosy as the bottoms of my feet. Standing in these radiating lines, I lift my arms as if passing through beams I imagine cast through the air. This is the place where every disparate thread of life is gathered to a single point. Here the acts of humanity do not seem out of place or garishly forceful. This is a thing that humankind has always quietly wished for, a way of living that does not obstruct the path of nature, or even more, is not at all different from it. We want an enduring relationship with our surrounding world. How the land holds up its end of the deal is difficult to describe in a place like this. What is here is a necessity that comes before food and shelter: the barest need of life, to be awakened.

I lose myself as I hold my arms flat to the plane of the eastern horizon. Humans are not orphans at this lacerated edge of the earth. We finally belong to the world.

The next day we move between the volcano and a stab of southerly mountains, walking onto the foot of an enormous dune sea. I pause there, where ropes of lava are taken under by the sand. Regan is eager to enter the strange and enormous shapes ahead of us. Even the earth is erased here, the black of lava sanded over. It is a lethally alluring place, utterly lacking in life, yet its dunes have the turning arc of DNA, and the slopes sink away with pleasingly organic curves. She tells me to come. Walk with her into the dunes.

It is not the same land I had been traveling on, too gentle and perfect. But when I step onto it, I realize that it is indeed the same. The world has eroded to this. Mountain ranges and canyons are reduced to their most elemental parts, broken from across the continent by ice, water, wind, and footsteps, turned to pieces so small that a storm could shape entire landscapes in a matter of minutes. The earth I had been walking across for all of these years had been turned to the shape of wind.

When we climb three hundred feet up the nearest sand crest, we look northwest and the dunes never end, flowing around each other like billowed cotton sheets sailing out and beyond the horizon. The dunes seem to take over the world. We move ahead, balancing on high dorsal fins, sending down elegant, liquid cascades of sand. When we stop, the wind frosts across our boots, coiling sand around our legs, trying to work our resistant bodies into the correct native shape of the dune.

For being so physical, it feels like a purely psychological place, a landscape of the mind. The wind and sand buzzes against my face so that there is no distance between my flesh and my thoughts and the farther landscape.

We arrive at the lip of a huge cauldron dropping between three high pyramids of sand where the wind turns, drilling downward. Great arcs of wind swirl around the circle, phantoms that sweep across us, catching on our chests and legs. The walls of this hole are steeply sloped and unmolested, smooth as the skin of a peach. Regan reaches down and unties her boots. The leather is squeaky. I do the same. It seems like a natural thing to do here, freeing ourselves. We strip our clothing and slide into this giant, convex dish, two naked bodies plunging down the slope, bringing avalanches of sand with us.

At the bottom of this cone, Regan's body blends sweetly into the shapes around her, her skin only a shade darker than the sand. Her breasts are neither small, nor large, nipples the color of almonds. She seems formed—her hips, her calves, the curve of her stomach matching exactly the arcs rising toward the dune crests high overhead. I kiss her. I kiss her closed eyes and her fingertips. I kiss the seductive, warm hollow beneath her throat and the plane of her breastbone. The slope of her back—my hand falling into the inward curve of muscles along her spine—is familiar, not at all like a first exploration. There is nothing startling. Her hair is as ordinary to me as wind. Fine hair on her forearms, and a tease of a few hairs trailing downward from her navel. I find the scars along her left shoulder blade, long, sinewy ridges from when she was once thrown from a horse into barbed wire. I follow them as if going through a map, knowing where I am, finding the other scars, one on her lower back, another below her right shoulder.

When her lips trace the edge of my ear, we slide into the sand, drawing each other down. We handle each other's bodies as if they are artifacts, sacred items found in the desert. When her back arches, I slip my hand beneath to support it, lifting the center of her body toward me. Her mouth barely opens, tasting the air, hands slowly fisting into the sand.

Each of us has a way of being. We have a shape, a process, a wish encoded into us. The dunes repeat themselves without end, certain profiles aligned unerringly with the wind. The canyons carve down with mathematic perfection. Even humans, with the exclusiveness we see in ourselves, are tugged by puppet strings of genetics and purpose, by the same demands written into the land. I have long wished to change myself, to erode into a grain, becoming a being of delicate comprehension, and at the same time to never leave the visceral, ravishing terrain of my origin, the blood, the rock, the sex, and the sky. So I came to this land transfixed.

When Regan and I lie still, her eyes are clear. She stares into me. Without speaking, she draws herself away, and I come to rest on my back. She stands, bending over to kiss my lips and then my right shoulder. Her body is now painted with a layer of sand, one grain deep across almost all of her skin. Seeing that I notice this, she looks down at herself and smiles. A desert animal. She turns and climbs out, sending banners of sand down to me. Our sliding footprints have already been removed by the wind, our presence reduced to this, two bodies alone in an empire of dunes.

Then there is only one body. She is gone. My eyes drift, coming to the apex over the hole. The sky is a painful blue. I do not want to alert my muscles. If I give the call to speak, no words will rise from my throat into my mouth. I am no longer a tool, no longer a thing that can be broken. The sun hovers at a far side of this round sky, a circle within a circle.

There has always been anguish and violence at these final places— charging seas, wind that rakes the mind, and ruptured, barren volcanoes. I have believed that because this land that I seek is terrible, because it tears at my eyes and my body, the end of it must be the most adverse thing imaginable. But it is not. It instead parts like a silk veil, slipping me into a realm as immeasurable and pure as birth.

Do you remember what it was like before you were born? Every person has that memory hidden at the boundaries of the mind. It was a time when you were everything, when you were not yet detached to drift separately from the world with your freed hands and legs. You expanded beyond your own body, a sensation that exceeded any physical nature that you have since come to know. Memory of it comes perhaps just as you are falling asleep, or at a rare moment of deep quiet, a feeling of neither peace nor fear. A sense beyond sense.

This is where this desolate land finally carries me, to the beginning.

A place before time, before my body and my mind. The most severe landscape has only one last ability: to remove, to tear down to the very start and to the end. My body slowly bakes, naked in the sun, the swallow of the dune hot against my skin. Whirlwinds scribble frenetically down the slopes toward me. They sizzle, picking up sand, skidding it across the surface, burying my fingers. Then my forearms. Sand gathers in the creases around my eyes, and in my navel. It sifts into my hair. It covers all of my scars until I am smooth.

In the bottom of this great parabola, far into a dune sea, I sink into the earth. One final privilege. I turn to sand.

Bibliography

Ambruster, Carol W., and Ray A. Williamson. "Sun and Sun Serpents: Continuing Observations in South-Eastern Utah." In *Archaeoastronomy in the 1990s*. Clive L. N. Ruggles, editor. Loughborough, UK: Group D Publications Ltd., 1990, pp. 219–26.

Billman, Brian R., Patricia M. Lambert, and Leonard L. Banks. "Cannibalism, Warfare, and Drought in the Mesa Verde Region During the Twelfth Century A.D." *American Antiquity* 65, no. 1 (2000): 145–90.

Binford, Lewis R. "Willow Smoke and Dogs' Tails: Hunter-Gatherer Settlement Systems and Archaeological Site Formation." *American Antiquity* 45, no. 1 (1980): 4–20.

Bowen, Thomas C. "A Survey of Archaeological Sites Near Guaymas, Sonora." *Kiva* 31, no. 1 (1965): 14–36.

———. *Unknown Island: Seri Indians, Europeans, and San Esteban Island in the Gulf of California*. Albuquerque: University of New Mexico Press, 2000.

Bowen, Thomas, and Edward Moser. "Seri Pottery." *Kiva* 33, No. 3 (1968): 89–132.

Carpenter, John, and Guadalupe Sanchez, editors. *Prehistory of the Borderlands: Recent Research in the Archaeology of Northern Mexico and the Southern Southwest*. Tucson: Arizona State Museum, 1997.

Childs, Thomas. "Sketch of the 'Sand Indians.'" *Kiva* 19, nos. 2–4 (1954): 27–39.

Clark, Jeffery J. *Tracking Prehistoric Migrations: Pueblo Settlers among the Tonto Basin Hohokam*. Anthropological Papers of the University of Arizona, Number 65. Tucson: University of Arizona Press, 2001.

Cordell, Linda. *Archaeology of the Southwest*. San Diego, Calif.: Academic Press, 1997.

Cordell, Linda S., and George J. Gumerman, editors. *Dynamics of Southwest Prehistory*. Washington, D.C.: Smithsonian Institution Press, 1989.

Crown, Patricia L., and W. James Judge, editors. *Chaco & Hohokam: Prehistoric Regional Systems in the American Southwest*. Santa Fe, N.M.: School of American Research Press, 1991.

Douglas, John E. "Autonomy and Regional Systems in the Late Prehistoric Southern Southwest." *American Antiquity* 60, no. 2 (1995): 240–58.

Ezell, Paul H. "An Archaeological Survey of Northwestern Papagueria." *Kiva* 19, nos. 2–4 (1954): 1–26.

Fay, George E. "A Seri Fertility Figurine from Bahia Kino, Sonora." *Kiva* 21 (1956): 11–12.

Felger, Richard Stephen, and Mary Beck Moser. *People of the Desert and the Sea: Ethnobotany of the Seri Indians.* Tucson: University of Arizona Press, 1991.

Fiedel, Stuart J. *Prehistory of the Americas.* Cambridge: Cambridge University Press, 1992.

Gumerman, George J., editor. *Themes in Southwest Prehistory.* Santa Fe, N.M.: School of American Research Press, 1994.

Hayden, Julian D. "Food Animal Cremations of the Sierra Pinacate, Sonora, Mexico." *Kiva* 50, no. 4 (1985): 237–48.

————. "Pre-Altithermal Archaeology in the Sierra Pinacate, Sonora, Mexico." *American Antiquity* 41, no. 3 (1976): 274–89.

————. "Hohokam Petroglyphs of the Sierra Pinacate, Sonora and the Hohokam Shell Expeditions." *Kiva* 37, no. 2 (1972): 74–83.

————. "A Summary Prehistory and History of the Sierra Pinacate, Sonora." *American Antiquity* 32, no. 3 (1967): 335–44.

LeBlanc, Steven A. *Prehistoric Warfare in the American Southwest.* Salt Lake City: University of Utah Press, 1999.

Malville, J. McKim, and Claudia Putnam. *Prehistoric Astronomy in the Southwest.* Boulder, Colo.: Johnson Books, 1993.

Malville, J. McKim, Frank W. Eddy, and Carol Ambruster. "Lunar Standstills at Chimney Rock." *Archaeoastronomy* 16 (1991): S43–S50.

McCluskey, Stephen C. "Lunar Astronomies of the Western Pueblos." In *World Archaeoastronomy: Selected Papers from the Second Oxford International Conference on Archaeoastronomy Held at Merida, Yucatan, Mexico, January 1986.* A. F. Aveni, editor. Cambridge: Cambridge University Press, 1989, pp. 355–64.

McGuire, Randall H., and Ann Valdo Howard. "The Structure and Organization of Hohokam Shell Exchange." *Kiva* 52, no. 2 (1987): 113–46.

McGuire, Randall H., and Michael B. Schiffer, editors. *Hohokam and Patayan Prehistory of Southwestern Arizona.* New York: Academic Press, 1982.

Moser, Edward, and Richard S. White Jr. "Seri Clay Figurines." *Kiva* 33, no. 3 (1968): 133–54.

Murray, W. B. "Calendrical Petroglyphs of Northern New Mexico." In *Archaeoastronomy in the New World.* A. F. Aveni, editor. Cambridge: Cambridge University Press, 1982, pp. 195–203.

Neitzel, Jill E., editor. *Great Towns and Regional Polities in the Prehistoric American Southwest and Southeast.* Albuquerque: University of New Mexico Press, 1999.

Reid, J. Jefferson, and David E. Doyel, editors. *Emil W. Haury's Prehistory of the Southwest*. Tucson: University of Arizona Press, 1986.

Reid, Jefferson, and Stephanie Whittlesey. *The Archaeology of Ancient Arizona*. Tucson: University of Arizona Press, 1997.

Stone, Connie Lynn. "Living in No Man's Land: Prehistoric Economic Strategies and Land Use Patterns in the Western Arizona Outback." Ph. D. diss., Arizona State University, 1990.

———. *People of the Desert, Canyons, and Pines: Prehistory of the Patayan Country in West Central Arizona*. Cultural Resource Series No. 5, Phoenix: Arizona State Office of the Bureau of Land Management, 1987.

Turner II, Christy G., and A. Jacqueline Turner. *Man Corn: Cannibalism and Violence in the Prehistoric American Southwest*. Salt Lake City: University of Utah Press, 1999.

Upham, Steadman. "Nomads of the Desert West: A Shifting Continuum in Prehistory." *Journal of World Prehistory* 8, no. 2 (1994): 113–67.

Villalpando, María Elisa. "The Archaeological Traditions of Sonora." In: *Greater Mesoamerica: The Archaeology of West and Northwest Mexico*. Michael S. Foster and Shirley Gorenstein, editors. Salt Lake City: University of Utah Press, 2000, pp. 241–53.

Whalen, Michael E. "Moving Out of the Archaic on the Edge of the Southwest." *American Antiquity* 59, no. 4 (1994): 622–39.

Acknowledgments

This book would not have been conceivable without the sly and strange masters that I have apprenticed under. I extend my thanks to them:

Sharon Riegel, my mother, who burns almost too hot and bright to be touched.

Laura Slavik, the sharp teeth and nails of truth, the purr of sound sleep.

Tom Vimont floating naked in a water hole, laughing like a giant, his voice vanishing off in the desert.

The cursing, growling brilliance of Nathan Waggoner, whose claws are sunk deep into the world, not letting go, not a chance.

The animal inquisitiveness of Irvin Fernandez, the first man to convince me that I must eat live insects, and that they must be chewed thoroughly.

Everyone at Sasquatch Books who saved my ass, who made publishing a thing I could swallow, including Gary Luke, my editor, who has taken me this far.

Elizabeth Redding, eyes wide with observance, pupils round and shining as Neptune.

Judy Ortega Smith and her well-founded optimism—ride the dragon, sweet woman.

Kim Malville, who first pried open the ancient box, allowing me to glimpse these deepest secrets, who grinned when talking of human hearts cut out still beating atop the Temple Mayor.

Dirk Vaughan who . . . who . . . can it ever be said?

His brother, Devin, body streaked in red paint, barefoot on the rocks, arms to the sky, eighty miles from the nearest road of any kind. I will follow you to the ends of the earth.

Sue Ware, the Bone Woman, Pursuer of Wolves, both Ph.D. and shaman, who reminded me of the ultimate lesson: Always Come Back.

Holly of the nimble fingers and Felix of certain hands.

Walt Anderson, who contains every last bit of the universe in his mind, and can somehow say it out loud with the voice of kindness.

The graciousness of Dick Moore and his study cluttered with maps, his mind made of sandstone and basalt.

Todd Roberston, the calm, wise beat to my life, and the steady protector of the land, remember our days . . . our weeks . . . on the Yukon, your hands dragging in the water as I fended Arctic terns away from your unconscious body with a paddle—that is true love.

Alyssa Van Schmus, any time you want to go back to the middle of nowhere, gnash your terrible teeth and roll your terrible eyes, I am there.

Ron Wagner, an arrow to its target.

Craig Israelson, if, for nothing else, the gleam of madness, the single, uncanny bean floating in the Tex when the rest of us have been flushed.

Keith Knadler, who hides throughout this book, but never appears once. Why? Because you are water, my friend. This book is soaked with your presence. You are the wildest one that I know. If I could take a piece of you and graft it into me, I would.

Josh Levy, the spinning needle on the compass, the man who taught me to sing in midnight parking garages.

Sivi Ruder. You are the goddess of all things, the seer of all hearts. I am an old bone, or a bit of cactus spine you've collected into your infinite nest of human secrets. I am honored to have been gathered by you.

George Steck, who tells me it is nothing grander than putting one foot in front of the other—but I've mulled through your equations, George, I've walked your routes, and I've cursed your name while hanging from a rope at a set of boulders and pour-offs that you said were "not much of a problem." One foot in front of the other? Hell, if that's all there is to it, I'm almost there.

Regan Choi, who is the thing that I seek, the wild, ceaseless beauty of stars, sand, water, and wind.

Darin MacGilivray and his blazing-eyed questions—should I wish a rattlesnake to bite you and answer your curiosity?

Master Colin Wann, the ghost, I bow to you.

Finally, my father, James Childs, who is forever—I miss you, you son of a bitch.

About the Author

Craig Childs was born in Arizona and has spent much of his life in the Four Corners region, mainly in Colorado. Every year he walks between 1,000 and 3,000 miles, generally in the Southwest United States, either performing research in water or archaeology, or simply walking to see what is there. Most of these miles are off-trail in deep wilderness, almost all of them in the desert. He now lives with his wife in a cabin sans indoor plumbing (but including solar electricity) in western Colorado between the Black Canyon National Park and the West Elk Mountains. He has a masters degree in Desert Studies from Prescott College in Arizona where he is an adjunct professor in field science.

Childs has written for *Outside, Audubon, Sierra, Backpacker, Arizona Highways, Fine Cooking,* and *High Country News* and is the author of six books of natural history and travel. He is a regular commentator for National Public Radio.